JOE BIDEN
UNAUTHORIZED
And the 2020 Crackup
of the Democratic Party

Joe Biden Unauthorized and the 2020 Crackup of the Democratic Party

By Mike McCormick

Cover: Joe Biden photo available in public domain.

Photo credit: David Lienemann, official White House Photo

Book design by Erik Weems

ISBN 978-1-7337146-6-2

https://joebidenunauthorized.com

https://15yearsadeplorable.com/

Fifteen Years A Deplorable LLC

JOE BIDEN

UNAUTHORIZED

And the 2020 Crackup of the Democratic Party

by Mike McCormick

This book is truth in search of an audience,
so I dedicate it to those who are reasonable
enough to read it from start to finish.

Acknowledgements:

I'd like to thank all the people who helped
me with my life and this book. You know
who you are — now, then, and always

CONTENTS

Forward

A Book for Our Time

Truth about our political leaders these days is hard to find, especially if you are, like me, a reasonable American disgusted by the ocean of BS we have to navigate to get it.

My case is a little different, though, because unlike most reasonable Americans, I actually worked closely with those political leaders. I was a stenographer in the White House Press Office for the Bush, Obama, and Trump administrations from 2002 to 2018.

It was an exciting job. History happened right in front of me. But then so did a lot of BS. I saw it and heard it firsthand. Much of it the media told you about, but some of it they didn't.

That's why I'm writing this book, to fill in that gap. And since I worked primarily for Vice President Joe Biden during the Obama years, I can tell you a lot about Middle Class Joe, the White House Optimist.

Talk about an ocean of BS.

That said, I have written, edited, and self-published this book to authentically relate what I heard and saw Joe Biden say and do when I was his primary stenographer from 2011 to 2017. Not everything is here, but what I consider the important stuff is. And I defy anyone —

especially Joe — to refute the facts I have herein presented.

Also understand I am offering you a raw truth, self-published memoir — my story, from my perspective — about a man who is right now campaigning to be our next president. Without the publishing services of Amazon and IngramSpark, I wouldn't be able to do this. So thank you Amazon and IngramSpark.

The bad news for Joe is I was there for his murky business in Ukraine; his firehosing of our taxpayer dollars to Honduran drug dealers; his humiliations by Vladimir Putin, Xi Jinping, and Recep Erdogan; and his pathetic mismanagement of the U.S. military withdrawal from Iraq.

Didn't you hear about any of that? Not surprised. Think the White House press were easy on Joe? I'll explain why.

The good news for Joe is he did a few things well — some, in fact, were downright ennobling. That's in here, too.

This is a weird time in our country. The House Democrats recently voted to impeach President Donald Trump over a phone call. I guarantee, as someone who was in Ukraine with Vice President Joe Biden, this book will raise significant new questions about what he knew and when he knew it concerning his sketchy son's sketchy business in sketchy Ukraine.

In my opinion, President Trump was right to request help in investigating Joe and Hunter Biden. I think you'll find the facts I have put together in support of that opinion are stronger than anything else reported to date.

If Joe is going to run for president, he can't hide his past. At least not the past I saw. Amtrak Joe has some questions to answer.

And please understand, in the original version of this book, I believed

Joe when he said he had no knowledge of Hunter's business in Ukraine. But after digging into transcripts and visitor logs from President Obama's WhiteHouse.gov website, I now believe Joe has been lying.

Democrats in Congress (and Mitt Romney) voting to impeach our president over a Joe Biden lie? Democrats in Congress self-destructing their integrity and trustworthiness over a Joe Biden lie? Time to write a book.

So here it is: *Joe Biden Unauthorized and the 2020 Crackup of the Democratic Party.*

Joe

CHAPTER ONE

J oe Biden walked into a trap.

It was August 2016, during a harried state visit to Ankara, Turkey, and Joe Biden, vice president of the United States, the man who had made bragging about his foreign policy experience a cottage industry, should have known better.

But he didn't because, well, he's Joe Biden.

And I say this with respect for all he's accomplished, but it is not in his DNA to know better. It's in his DNA to almost know better.

But only *almost*.

It's important to note here, too, that while his full name is Joseph Robinette Biden, Jr., no one ever calls him that.

It's also important to note hardly anyone refers to him by the prominent title he earned after 36 years serving his beloved Democratic Party — Vice President Joe Biden.

No, to most people the world over, he's Joe Biden.

And therein lies a wrenching truth for the Democratic Party that is also endeared to him: Joe Biden, God love him, is Joe Biden.

Great guy, vast experience at the highest levels of government, passionate about progressive causes, but Joe Biden will never be the leader of the Democratic Party or the president of the United States.

But don't for a second think he sees it like that, or ever will see it like that.

Joe Biden will drive himself hard to win the presidency in 2020 — harder than most people half his age — and he will almost get there.

Almost.

Because, the reasoning has to follow, if he's careless enough to get trapped in Turkey, plus so many other examples of carelessness and misconduct I've here included in this book, can he be trusted as the leader of his party? Or as president of our country, which, incidentally, makes him the leader of the free world?

I'd say that's a question best answered by voters. In my opinion, 2020 will not be kind to Amtrak Joe.

Or his Democrats.

And I'm not just talking about his gaffes, which to me are examples of the clumsiness we all share. No, what I'm talking about is carelessness, and in the case of his son Hunter's business in Ukraine, misconduct.

From what I've seen and heard in my years working for Joe Biden, carelessness is one of his defining characteristics.

But so, too, is love.

Joe loves his family and he loves Democratic politics, but he has been careless with both. He loves people and he loves the spotlight, but he has been careless with both.

But not by much.

Joe's talent at weaving those warring themes into his storied life of public service has set him far and above almost all of his peers.

Almost all his peers.

Ironically, I don't think the trap in Turkey that caught Joe was set with the intention of denying him the presidency, but when seen along with so, so many other examples of carelessness, it will be the end of the line for Amtrak Joe.

It was a trap sprung during a time and a place when Joe Biden thought he was in control, but wasn't. It was a trap sprung by a world leader Joe Biden thought he knew, but didn't. It was a trap sprung because Joe Biden was acting in good faith, and the other guy wasn't. But that's politics.

And sometimes family.

Politics, especially international politics, as Joe Biden well knows, is a dirty and occasionally deadly business, especially in the company of Recep Tayyip Erdogan.

A vice president with Joe Biden's foreign relations experience should have known that. He didn't. He wasn't cautious. He wasn't shrewd. He was Joe Biden, and he walked into that trap with the same oblivious self-confidence that sent Custer hurtling towards the finality of Little Big Horn.

Certainly, Joe Biden's advisors should have known better. They bear as much responsibility for his blunder as he does. But they didn't see it. Or if they did, they didn't let on that they saw it, crossed their fingers and hoped it would blow over — as had happened so, so many times before.

I saw it and said nothing. Just as I had said nothing on so, so many previous episodes of Bidenesque bungling.

Working for Joe Biden as his stenographer for six-plus years meant discretion was built into my job requirements. It was my duty *not* to say what I saw and heard unless it was within the boundaries of official business. But that duty with Joe ended in the winter of 2017.

And then one year later, after working as a stenographer in Donald Trump's White House, I left that job and wrote my first book, *Fifteen Years A Deplorable: A White House Memoir.*

I'm proud of that book and the tough truths it relates. It centered on my experiences from the inside with biased White House journalists, unreported shortcomings of the Obama White House, Hillary Clinton's hapless 2016 presidential campaign, and the genius of President Donald Trump.

This book is different. In it I focus specifically on one major American politician, Vice President Joe Biden.

I am not spewing hate — there's more than enough of that being done. On both sides. But I am writing the truth — the good and the bad. This isn't hearsay, this is "I say". These are the things I saw.

So if you care to know the tough but important truths about Joe Biden, Amtrak Joe, Middle Class Joe, a man who many Democrats believe can defeat President Donald Trump in the 2020 election, read on.

But please understand that writing those unflattering truths makes me a White House whistleblower, and as that person, who is putting my name on my story, telling the truth is the only witness protection I have.

And to be clear, I am not relating any sensitive national security information. Nothing I saw or heard at the White House was classified.

But what I am relating are unreported truths about Joe Biden, a deeply flawed politician who was granted leniency time again by deeply flawed journalists. Some would call that bias, and they'd be right. My bias is to report what truly happened to the best of my ability.

I think this leniency is also being extended to his youngest son, Hunter Biden. And as this story emerges, in all its hideous details (and it will) I defy *The Washington Post* and *The New York Times* to excuse themselves for missing/ignoring a story with national security ramifications that has been right under their noses.

As for Joe Biden blundering into his Turkish trap, one other guy, an American reporter, saw it the way I saw it and wrote critically of our vice president. Essentially, he saw what I saw: weakness.

It is the weakness Donald Trump and his supporters see, the weakness our international adversaries see, the weakness reasonable Americans should have the chance to see for themselves.

But two other journalists saw it differently and wrote stories minimizing Biden's weakness. In their minds, it was not the story of the day. And their view carried the coverage.

Over the years of watching White House journalists play their angles, I have learned there are the facts that get reported, thus ensuring credibility, and then there are *all* the facts, some of which are left unsaid.

And because so much reporting was so forgiving on the Obama White House, Joe Biden may not even understand how he was trapped in Ankara. Reporters often gave Joe the benefit of the doubt. In that instance, I saw them nod agreeably when his staffers offered the excuse Joe wasn't at his best because he was tired.

Or if he does understand his blunder, he probably thinks he got away with something. But he didn't. Or at least he shouldn't. Because like all modern political traps, there's a damning videotape, of the type that supersedes lenient reporting.

In my opinion, this videotape, if seen by American viewers, would bring Joe Biden's presidential run to a screeching halt.

That is, if his son Hunter Biden's behavior, so well documented in Peter Schweizer's book *Secret Empires: How the American Political Class Hides Corruption and Enriches Family and Friends,* and the Hunter Biden confessional article written by Adam Entous for *The New Yorker,* haven't already put on the brakes.

But more on that later. Because before you hear the particulars of that trap, you need to hear why I was there in the first place, why I saw a monumental Joe Biden blunder when a roomful of people saw it differently, and why I'm making it public now in this book.

Joe's Risky Business

CHAPTER TWO

Joe Biden made five trips to Ukraine from 2014 through 2017. I was with him for three. Hunter Biden wasn't on the plane for any. Whatever business he was up to in Ukraine, he did not fly in on his dad's plane to accomplish it, as he done on a trip to China in December 2013.

It's critical that Joe Biden's timeline in Ukraine be rendered accurately and honestly because it is the Bidens' dealings with Ukrainian natural gas conglomerate Burisma Holdings that was the impetus for the Democrat-led House of Representatives impeachment vote against President Trump.

Because from what I've seen, these verified facts have been either misreported or drastically underreported. The worst of the reporting, though, is the blind faith acceptance that Joe Biden knew nothing about and did nothing to promote Hunter's business in Ukraine.

First and foremost, it's important to understand that Joe Biden is a hero in Ukraine.

Snipers were murdering scores of pro-democracy protesters in the Maidan in Kyiv when Joe Biden called Ukraine's slimy president, Viktor Yanukovych, on February 20, 2014, and convinced him to halt the attack, thus ending the slaughter.

No one ever talks about that, and they should. With a phone call, Joe changed history for the better. Ennobling.

The next day, Yanukovych disappointed his puppet master, Vladimir Putin, and fled the country rather than face the justice Joe promised he was in for, and this opened Ukraine up for democratic reforms.

Joe often spoke about his high school summers spent as a lifeguard, now over 50 years later his phone call was lifesaving for hundreds, maybe thousands. In Ukraine, Joe is revered — deservedly so.

But within weeks, that country was soon involved in another crisis, with Putin's "green men" invasion threatening its stability. Once again Joe saw his chance to leap to Ukraine's rescue (and incidentally get payback on Putin for publicly humiliating him three years earlier, but more on that later).

And wouldn't you know, the Navy Reserve had on February 19, 2014, advised Hunter Biden that he had been discharged for testing positive for cocaine use, so he jumped into the pool alongside his dad.[1]

I guess he had some extra time on his hands.

It's also important to note that Joe and Hunter didn't own up to Hunter's discharge until October 2014, well after the hubbub over Hunter's appointment to the Burisma board died down.

It's widely documented Ukraine is one of the most corrupt countries in the world. I often heard Joe opine off the record when traveling on Air Force Two, when asked about the prospect of Russia taking over Ukraine, if Ukraine is unable to rid itself of its rampant corruption, he'd say, it doesn't matter who's in charge.

And if that was the case, and Joe knew it, knew it in his bones, as he likes to say, why in the spring of 2014 would his son Hunter suddenly decide it was a great location for a business opportunity?

Burisma

What exactly triggered Hunter to join the board of Burisma Holdings in Ukraine? And why was Burisma Holdings suddenly interested in Hunter Biden, a man with no experience in the natural gas industry, but who just happened to be the son of America's vice president?

Did Joe have a role in Hunter's business decision or set the table for it?

Joe was always bragging about his amazing relationship with his sons, so wouldn't you think a responsible father who understands diplomacy, national security, and spycraft — and who is also protective of his image as the vice president of the United States — would *dissuade* his reckless, addiction-prone son from doing business in Ukraine?

Not this time. Not Joe and Hunter.

As the Adam Entous' *New Yorker* article made clear, the Biden family knew for years about the irresponsible choices Hunter made time and again as a result of his addictions. They knew about and kept hushed and hidden Hunter's drinking binges, cocaine binges, and repeated failures at rehabilitation clinics, which accelerated in severity in 2010.

That means Joe knew.

Yet he refused to acknowledge that. All the while I worked for him, Joe spoke about his son as though he was an upstanding model citizen, a shining light of the community.

But it was all a gigantic lie.

Time and again I transcribed portions of Joe's speeches where he bragged about Hunter's exemplary work for the World Food Program, Hunter's accomplishments at Yale or Georgetown, how he was an officer in the Navy Reserve.

More than any other vice president I worked for, Joe Biden bragged about his kids and grandkids. That's Joe being Joe. No problem with that.

Unless it's a cover-up.

I didn't know Hunter, but I knew Joe. And I trusted him to be honest about his kids and grandkids, especially since he was speaking publicly as the vice president of the United States, which meant that I, as his stenographer, transcribed his statements into the official record of the Obama White House.

I've never met Hunter Biden. But I sure heard a lot about him from his dad. I believed Joe's characterization of Hunter then, but I sure don't now.

In his July 2019 *New Yorker* article Adam Entous has Hunter confessing on the record to heavy drinking and drug binges starting in 2010, but then denying that he had ever had sex with Lunden Alexis Roberts, who at the time had lodged a paternity suit against him.[2]

A subsequent court-ordered paternity test has confirmed that denial as a lie. Hunter fathered their child after the couple met at a DuPont Circle strip club, but was only willing to pay child support to his baby's mother after a protracted legal battle.

Those are now irrefutable facts.[3]

And if Joe was lying about Hunter then, why isn't he lying about him now? Where do the lies start and where do they stop?

My first trip to Kyiv with Joe was April 21-22, 2014, as fighting was raging between government forces and Russian-backed separatists in the Donbass region.

Danger was in the air.

So was a heap of U.S. assistance, courtesy of Joe Biden.

According to excellent reporting in Peter Schweizer's book *Secret Empires: How the American Political Class Hides Corruption and Enriches Family and Friends,* Joe's charge into Kyiv came less than a week after April 16, 2014, when he met in the White House with Devon Archer, a close business associate of Hunter Biden and Chris Heinz, John Kerry's stepson.

But there was more to this than was reported by Peter Schweizer and Adam Entous, and using my White House experience, I did some digging into the official records. I found there was more than just that one important meeting. First, let's start with the critical dates, April 15-16, 2014.

April 15, 2014, Joe started the day in the White House, but then traveled to Boston to give a speech commemorating the one-year anniversary of the Boston Marathon bombing.

(Later in this book, you'll read how that incident prompted an especially eerie incident involving Joe.)

But before Joe left for Boston, one of his staffers, at 11:30 a.m., confirmed the appointment for Devon Archer to enter the West Wing for a meeting with Joe the following day at 11:30 a.m. I think it's notable that the appointment was made only 24 hours in advance because immediacy connotes priority.

I derived the information of that Devon Archer appointment from the 2014 Secret Service visitor logs. Here's a screenshot of the Excel spreadsheet I downloaded off Barack Obama's "frozen in time" WhiteHouse.gov website.[4]

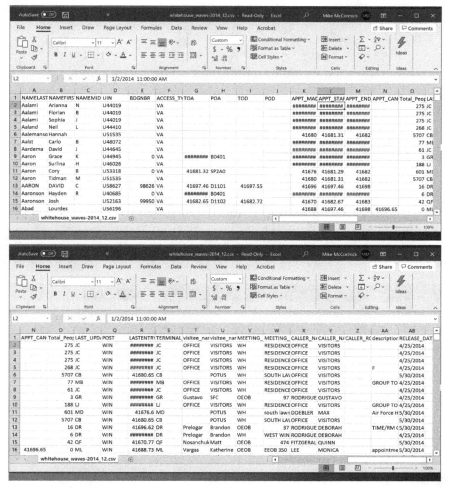

[Figure 1, above] 2014 Obama White House Secret Service Visitor Log.

Another thing about Joe's trip to Boston was that it was high visibility. So obviously it had been planned weeks in advance, which means that around the White House it would have been well known that Joe and most of his senior staff would be out of the building from midday into the evening of the 15th. That's not unusual.

But if someone in the West Wing wanted to have a critical meeting WITHOUT Joe or his staffers around, that would have been a good time for it. That is *unusual*.

And that's just what they did — in the Roosevelt Room.

Further examination of the Secret Service visitor logs indicates a meeting between President Obama and his political brain trust of Jim Messina, David Plouffe, and David Axelrod on April 15th in the Roosevelt Room at 4:30 p.m.

Here's another screenshot of the visitor logs I downloaded from Barack Obama's WhiteHouse.gov website.

[Figure 2, below.]

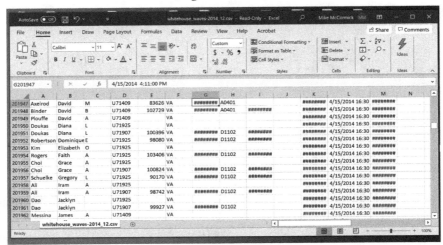

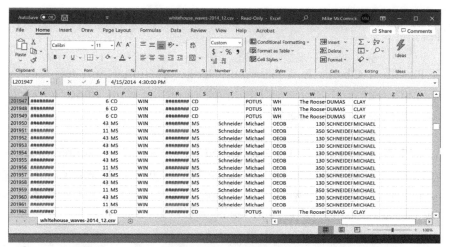

[Figure 2, above, continued] 2014 Obama White House Secret Service Visitor Log, Roosevelt Room, POTUS-et al.

Interesting timing for a critical Obama brain trust meeting excluding Joe, given the fact that he would be wheels up to Ukraine just five days later. He was being sent overseas on the important mission to give President Obama's answer to Vladimir Putin over his annexation of Crimea.

So, did President Obama and his advisors discuss the hot button issue at the time, Ukraine and Russia? Most certainly. Did they discuss the strategy for Joe's impending trip there? Most certainly. Did they discuss the aid package they were putting in place for natural gas development in Ukraine? Most certainly.

And where was Joe during their discussion about this critical trip? He was in Boston.

Hmmm.

Would President Obama have known about Hunter Biden's impending appointment to the board of Burisma Holdings, the Ukrainian natural gas conglomerate run by oligarch Mykola Zlochevsky before this meeting? Possibly.

If President Obama had prior knowledge of Hunter and Joe Biden's entanglement with Burisma Holdings, would he want advice about it from his brain trust? Possibly.

Would their discussion have solidified an objection to Hunter Biden's appointment to the board of Burisma Holdings, which was occurring almost simultaneously with his vice president dad winging into Ukraine with a big assistance package for energy security? Possibly.

But that's all conjecture. At least for now.

So let's return to the facts as contained in the Secret Service visitor logs. Here's another screenshot:

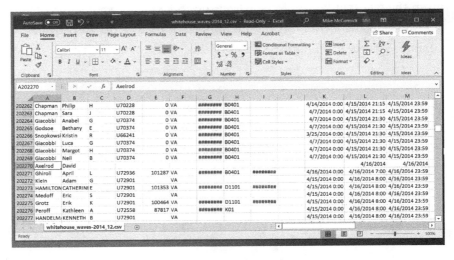

[Figure 3, above] 2014 Obama White House Secret Service Visitor Log, VPR, VPOTUS-David Axelrod.

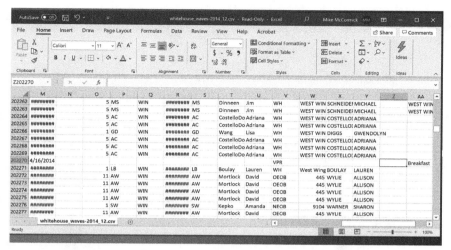

[Figure 3, above, continued] *2014 Obama White House Secret Service Visitor Log, VPR, VPOTUS-David Axelrod.*

As you can see, David Axelrod on the very next day, April 16th, bright and early, unusual for David, entered the VPR, which is the visitor log acronym for the Vice President's Residence, also known as NavObs, to have breakfast with Vice President Joe Biden.

Yes, correct, that David Axelrod. If you knew the Obama White House from the inside, as I do, you would note the oddity of David Axelrod battling D.C. morning rush hour traffic to travel to NavObs for an early Joe Biden meeting, especially only a few hours after having a confab with Jim Messina, David Plouffe and Barack Obama.

This tells me it was important for Axelrod to see Joe off the White House grounds, in the relative privacy of NavObs. This wasn't just an everyday meeting, which could be accomplished just a few hours later when Joe would be in the West Wing, anyway. No, this was something much more.

What message do we think David Axelrod was delivering to Joe Biden?

Hard to say, but I guarantee they talked about more than grandkids and golf.

And what's interesting is that Hunter Biden, who at the time only lived about a mile from NavObs, could have also been present at that breakfast meeting without it being documented in Secret Service visitor logs. As a family member of the vice president, he wouldn't need an appointment to pass through Secret Service checkpoints.

So was Hunter Biden having breakfast with his dad and David Axelrod on April 16, 2014?

No way to know unless they answer up about it.

Reading between the lines, this is a strange development in Bidenland. David Axelrod was no fan of Joe Biden's self-promotional tendencies. I'd say this breakfast meeting is evidence of his last-minute attempt to convey disapproval or warning.

Of course the only way to know for sure is to ask him.

So here it is: David Axelrod, in April 2014, did you meet with Vice President Joe Biden to caution him against plugging his son Hunter into the board of Burisma Holdings, a company that would directly benefit from the energy assistance package Joe was bringing to Ukraine?

And when/if you cautioned Joe, were you acting on orders from President Barack Obama?

And if David Axelrod did talk to Joe about Hunter and Ukraine, does that mean he should testify before the Senate to clarify what Joe knew and when he knew it?

And what about David Plouffe, Jim Messina, and Barack Obama? Should they testify before the Senate about what Joe Biden knew and when he knew it?

Because if those four men knew Joe Biden was manipulating taxpayer-funded energy assistance for Ukraine to benefit his son Hunter, that would be a big scandal for Barack Obama's administration, wouldn't it?

I'd say so.

But enough conjecture. Back to the facts.

Next timeline fact is the "timely coincidence" that Devon Archer, Hunter's business partner, was admitted to the West Wing to meet Vice President Joe Biden at 11:30 a.m., just a few hours after David Axelrod breakfasted with Joe.

So to break it down: The business partner (Devon Archer) of the vice president's son (Hunter Biden) and the secretary of state's stepson (Chris Heinz) met with the vice president in the White House a week before that vice president, Joe Biden, traveled to Ukraine with an emergency aid package — partly focused on improving energy.

Note that some reporting I've seen misconstrues Archer's visit as being on April 15th, but that's actually the date the appointment was made. So Devon Archer's meeting with Joe followed closely with Axelrod's. Here's the screenshot from the Secret Service visitor logs.

[Figure 4] 2014 Obama White House Secret Service Visitor Log, West Wing, VPOTUS-Devon Archer.

What could they have discussed?

And don't forget Hunter. Was he there at this meeting in his dad's office? Could have been. Again, while Devon Archer needs an appointment to enter the White House, Hunter does not.

In Adam Entous' reporting in the *New Yorker,* Devon Archer at the time of this hastily arranged meeting with Joe had admitted that he'd already been associated with Ukrainian natural gas oligarch Mykola Zlochevsky and Polish ex-president Aleksander Kwasniewski.

So if Joe was soon off to Ukraine with energy assistance for Burisma Holdings, wouldn't that be his reason for meeting with Devon Archer?

Bear in mind, Joe Biden had been hyping American assistance to Ukraine's natural gas industry since his first visit there as vice president in 2009. No doubt Hunter heard about it over the kitchen table. But then Joe and Hunter are both on the record as stating they never discussed Hunter's business with each other.

Really? Never?

All the more fishy that amidst these White House planning meetings, on or about April 18, 2014, Mykola Zlochevsky's Burisma Holdings, surreptitiously signed Hunter Biden and Devon Archer to its board of directors.

Nice timing on that and side-splitting funny because neither Hunter nor Devon knew anything about natural gas. *Or Ukraine.*

Chris Heinz, Secretary of State John Kerry's stepson, to his credit, moved quickly to sever business ties with Hunter Biden and Devon Archer upon learning they were the newest Burisma Holdings board members; that fact we have according to excellent reporting by *The Washington Examiner's* Alana Goodman.

What's interesting in that reporting is that Heinz learned about Hunter and Devon joining the board of Burisma Holdings through a press release that company put out May 13, 2014. That press release, tardy by several weeks, revealed the fact that Burisma Holdings was generously compensating Hunter Biden and Devon Archer, and thus became the starting point for press inquiries about the potential for a conflict of interest.

To me the significance of Heinz severing business ties with his two partners is that he learned about their new Ukraine venture in a press release. In other words, the trio never talked about such a sketchy move amongst themselves. It wasn't a business goal they had discussed in advance. Quite possibly it was just something that fell in Hunter and Devon's laps, and the minute Heinz heard about it in May 2014, he bailed. Smart guy.

So how did that lucrative opportunity arise for Joe's son and his friend but not for their business partner? And if so, from where did the idea of them joining Burisma Holdings' board originate?

Hunter Biden told the *Washington Post* that he was recruited to the Burisma Holdings board by former president of Poland Aleksander Kwasniewski, who was already a board member. So the *Post* did their job on that.

But why Hunter and Devon for the board? Why was Devon part of the package?

Adam Entous offers a partial answer with the revelation that Devon Archer told him Aleksander Kwasniewski recruited him to the board off a recommendation by Zlochevsky in early 2014.

But how early? Because Joe was in both Poland and Ukraine during that time, so was he directly or indirectly behind their recruitment?

These are important questions that I didn't see raised in anybody's reporting. So here's what I think happened based on what I witnessed.

In March 2014, Joe scrambled his staffers, including me, for a quickie trip to Poland and Lithuania to reassure Putin's nervous neighbors that Team Obama would not allow Russia to invade them as it was actually then still doing to Ukraine.

I recall that trip was fast and furious. After a long flight into Warsaw to see Prime Minister Tusk, Joe hustled through a series of meetings and press announcements before flying off to Lithuania for the overnight, followed by another high-speed day of meetings and speeches.[5]

Nonetheless, while in Poland there was plenty of time for Joe Biden to discuss his new pet project, Ukrainian energy security, with the ex-president of Poland, his pal Kwasniewski, who would have been the logical world leader to discuss that with because he was on the newly forming board of Burisma Holdings. The two men could have spoken on the phone before or after the trip, and there was ample opportunity on the ground during Joe's visit.

There is a noteworthy intersection between Joe and Kwasniewski through their joint work on the inclusion of Poland into NATO in the early 2000s and then later through Kwasniewski's faculty position at Georgetown University. Both Joe and Hunter were prominent Georgetown supporters.

When questioned, Joe states emphatically he never discussed Hunter's business directly with Hunter. But did he discuss it indirectly, like through a third party? Aleksander Kwasniewski maybe?

Because when Hunter Biden and Devon Archer were recruited to the board of Ukraine's up and coming, oligarch-run, natural gas conglomerate by Aleksander Kwasniewski, where was Joe?

On his way to Ukraine with U.S. assistance earmarked for energy security and the natural gas sector.

Hmmm.

So what was that energy assistance Joe was bringing to Ukraine? And was it the real reason for Hunter and Devon getting board seats?

Well, on the Air Force Two flight into Ukraine on April 21st, Jake Sullivan, Joe Biden's national security advisor, came to the rear of the plane where I sat with the handful of reporters who had signed up for the trip, including a crew from ABC News.

Jake's job, and he did it well, was to brief the press off the record as a senior administration official about the national security dynamics of the trip.

We were, after all, flying into a restive city at a turbulent time. Russian troops were mingled in with separatists in bloody skirmishes against Ukrainian troops in the Donbass. Vladimir Putin had strong-armed his way into Ukraine right under Team Obama's noses, and Kyiv was swarming with Russian operatives.

And Joe was there to help.

So, as I stood next to Jake, recording his every word for transcription, he explained on Joe's behalf, that while the Obama administration wasn't offering any lethal aid for Ukraine — guns, bullets, and missiles — they were offering to guarantee a massive loan from the International Monetary Fund, which was a big deal.

Oh, and energy assistance. They were bringing that, too. Here's Jake addressing that from that transcript I prepared of his Air Force Two brief.[6]

"[Vice President Biden] will speak about both the short- and long-term energy situation in Ukraine. As he arrives, there will also be a team on the ground from the United States, a team of experts working on the reverse flow issue. That team will be in Kyiv and then will travel also to Slovakia, Poland and Hungary to help address the issue of reversing the flow of natural gas to provide Ukraine with some measure of short-term supply of natural gas as they look to replenish their stores.

"But also he'll discuss with them medium- and long-term strategies to boost conventional gas production, and also to begin to take advantage of the unconventional gas reserves that are in Ukraine."

So now we know the *what*. But *why*, specifically, was it Joe Biden who was now charged with this very high-profile, critical task of rescuing Ukraine with energy security?

But first, here's another interesting tidbit from that briefing. And as much as I criticize some members of the press for their bias, this is an example of a reporter asking an astute question. I don't recall exactly who it was, but maybe they'll come forward and claim credit for it.

Here it is.

"Q Could you just say how this trip came about? Obviously the Vice President has a long history of diplomatic relations with Ukraine. Was this something that was his initiative? Did the President ask him to go because of those relationships? Or how did that come —

"SENIOR ADMINISTRATION OFFICIAL: The reason I'm pausing here is it's one of those -- it's one of those conversations where it's a little hard to say whether the President asked him or he said, I

want to go. It grew out of a conversation that the two of them had, and both of them agreed that it was important for the U.S. to send a high-level signal of support for all of the lines of effort that this government is undertaking."[7]

I've heard hundreds of these background briefings with senior administration officials. Every White House communications team I have worked with holds background briefings. It's a controlled conduit of off-the-record information fed to reporters who won't attribute what they hear at that time to a named White House official. They can, however, use that information later as they ask questions of White House officials who are speaking on the record.

I don't know why Jake chose to be off the record for this briefing. But in my opinion that's not as important as the question of how Joe wound up in charge. Because right now with the impeachment of a president hanging in the air, it's a very important question.

Ultimately, there were only two people involved in the decision that Joe Biden was to be the point man on all things Ukraine — Joe Biden and Barack Obama. And right then and there, Jake Sullivan had to split hairs on who made the call.

My opinion of why Joe Biden was heading Team Obama's "rescue" of Ukraine is that he wanted to position himself for this historical opportunity, and in the process plug his son and his son's pal into lucrative positions on the board of Burisma Holdings, which then directly benefited from the aid program he put in motion with the help of his friend Kwasniewski.

Then when Axelrod raised Obama's objection to that over breakfast, Joe ignored him.

Joe, you know a quid pro quo with taxpayers' dollars is a no-no. Talk about enabling your kid.

Wow.

At this point this is all conjecture, but it's my conjecture based on a factual timeline using evidence which until now has been unreported.

The easiest way to turn this evidence into proof is for the participants to explain themselves, preferably under oath before the Senate.

But wait, there's more!

Upon arrival in Kyiv just hours after the Sullivan briefing, Joe started a series of meetings with Ukrainian government officials and civil society groups. The following day he made a very revealing statement to the press, which included his full-throated support for an American "team" on the ground to assist Ukraine with its energy production. He said it in public, loud and proud.

Here's the quote from the transcript I prepared of Vice President Joe Biden's remarks to the press with then-Prime Minister Arseniy Yatsenyuk on April 22, 2014:[8]

> *"The Prime Minister and I also spoke about energy. An American team is currently in the region working with Ukraine and its neighbors to increase Ukraine's short-term energy supply. And I've been on the telephone with many of your neighbors, as you know, talking about the way to increase that supply. And teams are coming to support long-term improvements so that no nation — let me be precise, so that Russia can no longer use energy as a political weapon against Ukraine and Europe.*

"With the investments and right choices, Ukraine can reduce its energy dependence and increase its energy security. We will stand with you in every way we can for you to accomplish that goal."

Out of that statement, this is the question Joe should answer for reasonable Americans: Were you in your speech of April 22, 2014, using your office to promote your son Hunter's new benefactor, Burisma Holdings?

And what's more, I doubt the whistleblower whose objection to President Trump's phone call started the impeachment in the House was even on that trip with us. In which case, that person was uninformed as to the facts of Joe Biden's activities in Ukraine, and thus irresponsible in their communications to the inspector general.

I argue that if the whistleblower heard that April 2014 speech and those briefings and understood them as I do, there would have been no impeachment.

An embarrassing investigation of Joe Biden, yes. But an impeachment, no.

A political speech which offers a few actual facts, as opposed to all the billowy, idealistic hype, is a rarity. And here was Joe laying out an actual fact that there was an American "team" on the ground and more on the way.

So were Hunter and Archer one of those teams? Wow, if Hunter Biden's birthday is April 22nd, he got a doozy of a gift from Dad. And his buddy Devon Archer was in on it.

Was Joe promoting Hunter Biden and Devon Archer when he said "teams are coming to support long-term improvements"?

And were Joe's calls to Hungary, Poland, and Slovakia *"about the way to increase that supply"* on behalf of the citizens of the United States and Team Obama; or Team Hunter Biden/Burisma Holdings; or all of the above?

Maybe Joe will recommend the American public see the transcripts of THOSE calls, especially since Aleksander Kwasniewski may have been the recipient of one. *Then again, maybe not!*

I do recall on a later trip to Ukraine, a reporter asking Vice President Biden face-to-face about Hunter's business there.

Justin Sink — remember that name — one of the mumbliest reporters on the White House beat, had written an excellent story for *The Hill* newspaper on Hunter and Joe's affiliation with Burisma Holdings — including a denial by Joe's people that he knew about Hunter's business dealings — when the company publicly announced Hunter's board appointment in their May 2014 press release.

On a later trip to Ukraine, he put that question directly to Joe on the street in Kyiv. Credit Justin with being bold enough to challenge a vice president with a tough personal question.

Biden drew himself up, put on his sternest judiciary committee chairman face, and declared that his son was a private citizen and he never spoke to him about his business endeavors.

Official question, official answer. Done.

I was standing right there and I believed Joe then, but I don't now. Not after all that is coming out about Joe and his family covering up for Hunter's addiction.

I also recall Joe bragging about personally withholding American aid, about a billion dollars' worth, from Ukraine as a way to get a man he considered very corrupt fired from his job as a prosecutor. This was revealed in an August 2016 interview conducted by Steve Clemons of *The Atlantic,* which mirrors the statement he also famously made in 2018 on a televised forum with the Council on Foreign Relations.

This is the statement President Trump thought needed digging into because what Joe never bothered to mention in either instance was that the fired prosecutor was allegedly looking into corruption by Hunter Biden's benefactor Burisma Holdings.

The truth will out on that, as well.

To date, Ukraine has not found any evidence of impropriety by Hunter Biden during his tenure with Burisma Holdings, from which he separated in early 2019. But, at President Trump's insistence, they are digging into it. And they should be.

Joe is devoted to his family, but entwining his vice presidency with his sketchy son's sketchy business venture was more than careless.

At an October 2019 press conference in the White House, President Trump described the Bidens as "stone cold crooked," and on this I agree with him.

I don't believe Joe Biden will ever admit Hunter's Burisma Holdings board appointment was a quid pro quo for U.S. energy assistance, at least not on the record. That would make him a self-serving elitist. Not a good fit for his "Middle Class" Joe brand.

But who were the *"teams"*, Joe?

Estimates are that Burisma Holdings paid over $3 million to companies controlled by Hunter Biden and Devon Archer.

Were they one of the "teams" Joe was promoting? Sure looks that way to me.

On the day Hunter Biden and his buddy Devon Archer tied in with Burisma Holdings, Joe Biden showed up in Ukraine with U.S. energy assistance benefiting it; and then later Joe personally shuts down a pesky investigation threatening it.

Quid Pro Quo Joe.

Joe Biden on many occasions proffered Justice Brandeis' famous quote "sunlight is the best disinfectant" as a finger-wag at his opponents' misbehavior. I now believe those words are destined to haunt both him and his Democratic Party in 2020.

Because in my opinion the meeting with President Obama, David Axelrod, David Plouffe, and Jim Messina evolved into an Obama White House cover-up of Joe Biden promoting Burisma Holdings as a quid pro quo for that company giving his son Hunter a lucrative position on its board.

And if that is, indeed, the case, reasonable Americans will demand it be investigated, and that will not play well for the Democrats as they face election in 2020 or history ever after.

If Barack Obama, David Axelrod, David Plouffe, and Jim Messina KNEW in April 2014 the Joe Biden was corrupting his vice presidency (and their administration) to enrich his son, and they withheld that knowledge from their Democratic colleagues as they pursued the impeachment of President Donald Trump in 2019-2020, they have the sown the seeds of destruction of their Democratic Party.

And if they KNEW and TOLD their Democratic colleagues in Congress the truth about Joe Biden's corrupt activities, and the House Democrats pushed for the impeachment of President Trump anyway, that's even worse — the politics of blind hatred smearing a sitting president and his voters.

(See Chapter 10: *The Greatest Joe Biden Speech You Never Heard* for George Washington's take on such a political conspiracy.)

However President Obama and his team played it, when the sunlight hits this tawdry episode in our nation's history, and it will, reasonable American voters will punish the Democratic Party at the 2020 Election — up and down the ticket.

Bitch Slapped in Moscow

CHAPTER THREE

The first vivid personal memory I have of Joe Biden occurred at Joint Base Andrews as I was boarding his blue and white Air Force Two for my first overseas trip with him in March 2011.

There I was, trudging up the aluminum boarding stairs at the front of the plane, hefting my heavy stenographer's equipment case, then once inside, skirting respectfully past the vice president's cabin and realizing he was already in there holding forth with some of his senior staffers because I heard him bellow emphatically and unmistakably, *"give me a fucking break".*

It was not my first time on Air Force Two. I had traveled often on that very same plane with Vice President Cheney when I worked as his stenographer from 2002 to 2007. But it was certainly the first time I'd heard anyone on Air Force Two drop an F-bomb, let alone have it be the vice president of the United States.

Joe Biden, God love him, is Joe "BFD" Biden.

We were loading in for a trip to Vladimir Putin's Russia. The goal was to promote Team Obama's vaunted Russian "reset", but instead, from what I witnessed, it became an unreported truth as to how Putin viewed Joe Biden, the Russian "reset", and Team Obama.

Even though Dimitry Medvedev was then the Russian president, there was no question that engaging with Putin, then the prime minister, was Joe's objective because it was clear then and still is that Putin is in charge of Russia.

Given the way he treated Joe Biden, Putin was in charge of him, too.

At that point in time in the Obama administration, Joe Biden was following up — some would say riding the coattails — on Hillary Clinton and Barack Obama's initial visits to Russia as they promoted the "success" of Obama's Russian reset, a term Biden first coined at the Munich Security Conference in 2009.

This trip was Joe's turn, and it was a big deal for him. He had been itching for a one-on-one shot at Vladimir Putin for a long time, probably dating back to when President George W. Bush in 2001 had described looking Putin in the eye and getting a sense of his soul.

It was a tricky time for President Obama. His Democrats had been ravaged in the midterm elections only a few months earlier. Obama described the results as the *shellacking* it was.[9]

By historic margins, Tea Party candidates had returned the House to Republican control largely on domestic issues. So to right their wobbly ship of state, Team Obama had a brilliant idea: Have Joe Biden meet Vladimir Putin!

To our Corvette-revving vice president, that meant one thing and one thing only: It was about time they let him be in the driver's seat for a high-profile meeting with Putin. Judging by the boisterous mood on the plane, Joe Biden was raring to go.

Though I was part of the traveling staff assigned to Air Force Two for both

Vice President Cheney and Vice President Biden, my support position was about three levels removed from them. The vice presidents and their senior staffers certainly did not know me by name and only recognized me by proximity to staffers they did know.

Nonetheless, being amongst the staff, and getting briefed down to my level often gave me hints as to the thinking at the top. On this trip, the thinking at the top was that Joe Biden was not going to allow Vladimir Putin to dominate him in the way Putin had done to Barack Obama.

I recall Biden staffers emphasizing to me how Obama's first encounter with Putin, a 2009 one-on-one meeting in Russia, had been an hours-long lecture about the dishonesty of the Bush administration, which Putin delivered with such vehemence that Obama couldn't get a word in edgewise.

The takeaway was that Obama for the entirety of this critical meeting had said next to nothing — either because he silently agreed with Putin about his predecessor, which is never a good starting point for a U.S. president. Or more simply, Putin had gone KGB on him and "disinformationed" him out of a "conversational" of equals.

From what I gathered, Joe Biden was confident he could go nose-to-nose with Vladimir Putin and show him and Barack Obama how it was done. Biden, as he was quick to remind people, had been traveling to Moscow as a senator and dealing with Russian leaders since the Cold War days of Leonid Brezhnev.

The duty I was to perform for Vice President Biden on the trip was to record and type his public words and any interactions he had with the press for the official White House transcript of record.

It was a simple act, valued for its integrity. Hear the words, record the words, type the words without opinion, embellishment, or omission. Render them accurate for history and informed debate. Which any reasonable person would agree is an important task for our democracy.

Especially when those words are spoken by Joe Biden, Flub King Extraordinaire.

So, I definitely had my work cut out for me, not that I minded. Because at the time I was not a White House employee, but a contractor — an experienced one at that.

As I said earlier, I had flown on Air Force Two and Air Force One during my first stint as a White House stenographer from 2002 to 2007. After a brief interlude as a communications director for a Richmond, Virginia nonprofit, which ended because of job loss in the downturn of 2009, I returned to the White House Stenographers Office in 2010.

And while I do hold medium-rare conservative views on subjects like the economy, foreign policy, law enforcement, efficient government, and my personal responsibility to my fellow citizens and theirs to me, I was enthusiastic about working for Barack Obama and Joe Biden, despite surface political differences. The same held true for my good friend and mentor, the then director of the White House Stenographers Office, a woman I will refer to as "CD" for Cheerful Director.

CD had started as a White House stenographer the day after the bombing of the Marine barracks in Beirut in 1983, and since then had moved up the ranks.

She was the director who first hired me into the White House in 2002. We were contractors at the time. Thanks to her integrity and work ethic, our office was held in high esteem in the Bush White House by the staffers we worked with and the press who covered them. President Bush called us the *"Mighty Stenos."*

For most of my time with CD, we shared a great team spirit, which was important because long hours and an unpredictable schedule are the hallmark of a White House position.

So, having returned to D.C. from Richmond, CD told me they had an opening if I was interested. I jumped at the chance to work for her in the White House once again.

So from April 2010 through the inauguration of President Donald Trump, I added my experience to Barack Obama's White House.

That said, in the Obama years I kept my politics largely to myself. Any disagreements I had with his policies were nobody's business but my own. It was always my duty and honor to give President Obama and Vice President Biden the best of my effort and talent.

I also gave President Bush and Vice President Cheney my best when I worked for them, and as well for President Trump and Vice President Pence when I worked for them.

But then in early January 2011, there was a shift in our office. CD told me she needed a more experienced hand to cover Vice President Biden, who was quite the challenge. She asked if I would replace the guy who was struggling and agree to become the vice president's sole stenographer.

I accepted for two reasons. One, it would give me more family time since I was obligated to travel with Vice President Biden only on international trips, about once every three months or so.

The other reason was that as contractors in the White House, our customer service had to be better than the best. I could see CD's point that we needed to step up our game for Vice President Biden. Winning a contract is a competition, and that requires your absolute best.

Even though my duties split me off from the group for a lot of off-hour, solitary office work, I knew I was the best choice to handle the challenge.

So, then a few months later, in March 2011, I found myself winging my way to Moscow with Joe Biden.

From my past experience, I was surprised to be included in the trip because there was only one journalist in the traveling press pool, a print reporter, Jonathan Weisman, from *The Wall Street Journal.* Usually my services were only required if there were three or more journalists on the plane. But I was told by the vice president's communications team they wanted me there because more Moscow-based journalists would be added to the press pool once we arrived. *Plus* the topics were sensitive, so they wanted transcripts ASAP.

The pre-trip security brief was sobering. Don't bring a cellphone, it will be compromised. Don't connect any of your devices or computers to the internet through host nation portals, they will be compromised. Listening devices and video cameras are monitoring you 24 hours a day, act accordingly. *Enjoy your stay in Moscow.*

In addition to bragging about the "reset", Joe Biden was going to discuss how the Obama administration viewed Russia's accession to the World Trade Organization, something Vladimir Putin very much wanted. He was also going to talk about human rights with Russian nongovernment organizations and political reform with opposition leaders. There would be a business roundtable in Skolkovo, the purported Silicon Valley of

Russia, and a lengthy speech at Moscow State University.

While the public face of Biden's trip appeared packed with good intentions, it was also designed to "guide" Putin's future ambitions to align better with the world vision of Barack Obama, who obviously considered himself an authority on international relations, having won the Nobel Peace Prize a little more than a year before.

Thus, the trip's main event was undoubtedly the meeting between Vice President Joe Biden and Prime Minister Vladimir Putin at the Russian White House, a large white, quite drab building in Moscow that houses the Russian Prime Minister's Office.

In a number of ways the Russian White House was a good setting for the meeting with Putin. It's the building Russian army tanks shelled under orders from Boris Yeltsin in October 1993 to eliminate a rival faction's claim to power. Dead politicians, blood in the streets. That's Mother Russia for you, when they roll, they do it with tanks.

I recall it being a tense motorcade ride to the Putin meeting from a morning discussion the Vice President had with leaders of Russian civil society groups. We had a police escort and were zooming high speed, no stops past the Kremlin, Lenin's Tomb, and thank God, a McDonald's.

The history buff in me was delighted the city was carpeted in snow. To understand Russia, you'll want to see Moscow during winter — its beautiful, pitiless winter.

After a brief "grip and grin" that had Putin and Biden posing for official photographers in front of the American and Russian flags, the decisive meeting began with formal statements in front of a bevy of journalists, photo, print, and television, most of whom were based in Moscow.

I have over the years been in hundreds of these world leader one-on-ones. Rare is the politician who doesn't want to look their best when they're hosting another world leader, so the media is always in on at least the congenial part of it.

These are usually fairly benign events, sanitized of controversy and carefully choreographed so that the message is overwhelmingly of mutual respect, gravitas, and cooperation.

In the White House, our presidents conduct their one-on-ones in the Oval Office, though they will sometimes use other venues as well. The imagery of the dignified proceedings accentuates the strength of the world leaders' words.

Well, the room Vladimir Putin chose for his meeting with Joe Biden was an ornate, richly furnished but windowless conference room — so no natural light — just a bit bigger than a double-wide trailer.

A battery of television cameramen, complemented by several lighting technicians with portable lights, were clustered at the far end of the room. Associated Press and Reuters, the two main wire services for American media, had reporters there.

A long conference table, around which were seated about a dozen people, ran down the center of the room. On one side sat Vice President Biden and his delegation, facing them were Prime Minister Putin and his delegation.

I walked into the room with the White House travel pool from a doorway opposite the bank of photographers and videographers, and upon reaching the room's midpoint, I flattened myself against the wall to stay out of their shot.

My handheld microphone was turned on, my digital recorder was turned on. I knew this because I was listening to the room noise through earphones. My job was to record everything that happened in that room until Joe Biden finished speaking to the press. Then and only then would I leave.

I was with a small group of White House staffers and our traveling reporter, Jonathan Weisman. We positioned ourselves directly across the table from Biden, who sat at a distance from us of about 12 feet. Putin was seated with his back to us, probably about five feet away.

And while I could clearly hear each man and more importantly their translators through my headphones, I could also hear that the room acoustics were well amplified. The table was fitted out with elegant microphones for every attendee and loudspeakers were built into the walls.

The meeting started without a hitch, Putin, through a translator, spoke first, welcoming Biden. By his shirtless publicity photos, Putin obviously likes to fish. Apparently he's good at it because with Joe Biden, he knew exactly what bait to use.

After opening with an invitation for Joe to tell everyone his past experience in Russia, which Putin knew would prompt a long winded response, the ex-KGB officer sprung a surprise and proposed a visa-free travel regime between Russia, the European Union, and the United States to which Biden blurted out, "Good idea".

No, not a good idea, Joe, because clearly it was a gotcha offer.

As if the Obama administration was ever going to let hordes of Russian nationals roll into our homeland visa-free and essentially unchecked.

Please.

Or for that matter, into the EU ... or their neighbors the Baltics and Ukraine...

Umm, well, anyway.

So there was Biden, determined not to be dominated, offering his cheery stamp of approval to an outlandish Putin proposal.

Putin carried on, offering a few crumbs of praise for the improvement in U.S.-Russia relations, plus a bit of bragging on his mafia-state's growing economic stature.

Then it was Joe's turn.

Joe Biden is a savvy politician. He's an intelligent and experienced speaker, but he all too often unleashes self-aggrandizement at the cost of probity. In other words, he's a blowhard.

Joe made his points. First, pushing back on Putin's gotcha proposal by saying the decision was above his pay grade. So a save for Joe.

And then he effusively praised the reset, emphasizing it was his idea. Ego much, Joe?

But then came the part that, in my opinion, has always separated Joe Biden from the presidency and will always separate Joe Biden from the presidency, he took policy too far into his own legacy.

With Vladimir Putin looking impassively on, Joe Biden started in on a lecture about his decades-old part in U.S.-Russian negotiations with the dreaded phrase, "I've been around a long time".

Big mistake. Putin had baited his hook and Joe was caught.

He got about one sentence further into that spiel when — BAM — off went his microphone, off went the lights for the TV cameras, and stern Russian voices were commanding the press to leave.

And leave they did. Quickly, efficiently. Videocameras popping off of tripods. Tripods snapping shut. Portable lights clattering down retractable poles. No one spoke. No one lingered.

That was Putin in all his KGB ruthlessness. Whether by some prearranged signal or simply an undisclosed time limit, he had pulled the plug and done the unthinkable: he'd stolen Joe Biden's audience and rendered him speechless. Just shut him down in mid-sentence with the flick of an invisible switch.

Across the table, I could see Vice President of the United States Joe Biden, in the now dimly lit room, looking as duped as an exhausted fish in the bottom of a boat. No protest, no complaint. No, hey, I wasn't finished. Nothing.

But to me, the revelation was the premeditated precision of the snub. Putin, or more likely his henchmen, had plotted it out, probably long before this day began. They knew exactly what bait to use, exactly how Joe Biden would take it, and then when he did, they reeled him helplessly in.

Vladimir Putin and his delegation sat calmly and coldly as their American counterparts realized their blustery leader's big moment had been stolen right out from under him. The most powerful man in Russia had neither fear nor respect for Joe Biden. He had just played with him for sport.

That's what I saw. But American voters didn't get to see it like that.

Make no mistake about it, Vladimir Putin had just delivered a public humiliation — I'd call it a bitch slap — to Joe Biden, Team Obama's foreign policy expert. His message was unmistakable: I'm in charge of the room, I'm in charge of my country, and I'm in charge of the reset.

What American voters did hear was Team Obama's version of these events.

Biden would later on several occasions brag to supporters and members of the press of his candid exchange with Putin, which he says came in a wrap-up after the big meeting.

Only recently in his book *Promise Me, Dad* did he describe that meeting as "contentious". At least he finally came clean about what I saw, though it only took him six years.

Joe's self-promotional version of the interaction always centered on his momentary appraisal of Putin. Maybe you've heard it before. He has certainly put it out there often enough. I've typed it into transcripts more than a few times.

After praising Putin's magnificent office, which Biden teasingly attributed to Russia's growing acceptance of capitalism, he looked Putin in the eye and said something to the effect of, *I don't think you have a soul,* to which he said Putin replied in English, *good, then we have an understanding.*

With no press in attendance, we must take the Vice President at his word for that exchange. I wasn't in that part of the meeting, so there's no transcript of those remarks.

That's not unusual. My stenographer position was in support of the press office and the press office only, so I was present for transcription only when journalists were present and hearing statements and/or asking questions.

Note-taking of a nonpublic meeting behind closed doors would be done by staffers who were not compelled to share it with the public.

Putin has never confirmed or denied Biden's version of the exchange. To me, his belligerent actions toward Team Obama were the *real story.*

And that was the exact opposite of the happy hype Joe and Barack peddled right up until Putin's "green men" invaded Ukraine in 2014.

And now that Barack Obama's dealings with Vladimir Putin have been in rearview mirror for three years, does any American voter still believe our ex-president had a clue about what Putin was really up to?

How about Joe Biden?

And that begs the question, if Joe gets further down the road with his candidacy, is he the man Americans should trust to take on Putin?

What would you do, Joe, propose a *reset* to the *reset?*

And until now, did anyone outside of that room hear about Putin's brutish snub of Middle Class Joe, the White House Optimist?

Did anyone read about it in the **Washington Post** or the **New York Times?** Reuters was there, Associated Press was there.

Not a single Russian-based correspondent in that press pool reported that embarrassing tidbit through their outlets. No public news reporting I've seen or heard since referred to Putin shutting Biden down mid-sentence.

Imagine if that was Vice President Pence or Cheney (neither of which would ever be stupid enough to allow Putin to embarrass them like that). I guarantee the coverage would have been broad and unflattering.

Imagine if President Obama had pulled a stunt like that on Putin in the Oval Office. Obama fans Rachel Maddow and Stephen Colbert would still be crowing about it.

To his credit, Jonathan Weisman reported it as the insult it was. Once outside the meeting room, as the press pool gathered itself to go to a working area, he wisecracked to me, *"Joe Biden gets gonged. Twice."*

He was referring, of course, to the late '70s television comedy, *"The Gong Show"*, a satirical talent show, in which talentless performers were literally gonged off the stage by a panelist smacking a huge gong. Good, clean public humiliation fun.

For a **Wall Street Journal** reporter to say that about Joe Biden was pretty significant. And then he wrote a pool report about it. So he did his part.

I know he wrote it in the pool report which was released to every news outlet and journalist that covers White House because he told me how an angry Tony Blinken, one of Biden's key advisors on the trip, had berated him for his "snarky" pool report.

But when that pool report was read by news organizations back in States, bupkis. Nothing. Nada.

Maybe they didn't see it because of the time difference between Moscow and the U.S. Maybe their news judgement is different than mine. Maybe there were other stories of more immediate importance.

The Tea Party-infused Congress was just then negotiating a budget deal with the Obama White House, and Joe Biden was playing a key role in the negotiations via secure cellphone from Moscow while at the same time he was interacting with Putin and Medvedev. So maybe that's what the story was for the American media.

Jonathan Weisman, with whom I only spoke briefly once more after our return to Washington, did not get a one-on-one interview with Joe Biden on the flight back to the States. Nine hours on the plane and Joe Biden did not even grant a 15-minute sit-down with reporter who had spent a lot of time and effort (not to mention the money the **Wall Street Journal** ponied up for his travel pool seat) to follow him around Moscow, plus Finland and Moldova, the other two stops on our trip.

Jonathan had been a regular **Wall Street Journal** reporter in the White House Briefing Room from early in Obama's administration, but then he wasn't. Within a few months of our return from Moscow, he was off the beat.

He may or may not have more to say about his *"Joe Biden gets gonged in Moscow"* reporting. It was a long time ago and memories sometimes fade. And things change.

I bumped into him at a White House holiday press reception in December 2011, and he told he had left the **Journal** to go work for the **New York Times.** It was a brief conversation. I didn't ask the reason he left.

And that would be the last time I ever saw him in the White House. But I never forgot his wisecrack, *"Joe Biden gets gonged in Moscow. Twice."*

Here's my transcript, clearly, it ends with Joe in mid-sentence.[10]

> *The White House*
>
> *Office of the Vice President*
>
> *For Immediate Release*
>
> *March 10, 2011*
>
> *Remarks by Vice President Joe Biden*

and Russian Prime Minister Vladimir Putin

The White House

Moscow, Russia

12:46 P.M. (Local)

PRIME MINISTER PUTIN: (As translated.) Mr. Vice President -- (inaudible) -- there are quite a few things to enjoy in Moscow. And you haven't been here for quite a while. Since you've been here last time, and over this period of time, Moscow and Russia has changed a lot, and for the better I might add.

VICE PRESIDENT BIDEN: I would agree.

PRIME MINISTER PUTIN: (As translated.) You might be interested in getting to know Russia better, visiting other sights and cities. And on top of that, the relationship between our two countries has been developing quite well. Last year, the (inaudible) Russia has grown by 29 percent.

Turning -- we have completed several important things, including seeding for and verification of START III, and the peaceful use of nuclear energy. And the major American companies are doing business in Russia and are doing well. To name a few, General Electric, Boeing and Chevron -- virtually all the biggest companies are here.

And it is especially pleasing for us to witness the rise of the presence of big Russian investments between -- again, we are very pleased and very thankful to you for the fact that this has been -- (inaudible) -- and very sensitive areas such as I referred to earlier, use of nuclear energy. And I'm pleased with the fact that all of it has been passed through the procedures of the Foreign Investment Commission, and we are grateful for you for that to happen.

Again, it was very obvious to see the (inaudible) between the U.S. and Russian people is on the right track.

Currently, we are in the process of negotiating the possibility of the visa-free exchange between Russia and the countries of the European Union. The fact of the matter is, the U.S. enjoys this visa-free regime of exchange with virtually all of those countries in Europe.

This will be an important step in development of the Russia-U.S. relationship if we work first to introduce this visa-free regime of exchange between U.S.-Russia rather than European Union and Russia.

VICE PRESIDENT BIDEN: Good idea.

PRIME MINISTER PUTIN: (As translated.) Let's look to break all the outdated stereotypes concerning Russia and the U.S. Thus we have turned over a very substantial part of our history during this stage and we have started to have everything new. That would support absolutely before the -- in the relationship between Russia and the U.S.

And with this positive relation on your part, Distinguished Mr. Vice President, such an important person in the U.S. administration with clout (inaudible).

VICE PRESIDENT BIDEN: Mr. Prime Minister, in case you haven't noticed, there's a real difference between being President and Vice President. The very good news is the President and I agree 100 percent on the need to continue to establish a closer and closer relationship.

That's why the very first foreign policy annunciation our administration made was when I made the speech in Munich that it was time to push the reset button and change the atmosphere.

I would view the previous eight years -- did not take advantage of the opportunities that exist for both our countries. It does not really matter how -- it's in our self-interest and I hope in the self-interest of Russia to have our relationship grow.

I've made one observation the last two years, when other countries around the globe have a problem they either go to Moscow or Washington. They don't want to go to the other capitals.

We have an opportunity to build on this over the years. Not only on New START, cooperation in Afghanistan, cooperation on drugs, cooperation in -- a whole range of other areas -- now is the time to focus on the economy.

You mentioned Boeing; yesterday, I met with a group of American and Russian CEOs -- conference. A Russian -- the chairman of a Russian organization, I'll not state it, said that there was reason for American companies to be here because the markets are here and named some other reasons why it was in the interest of American companies.

The chairman of Boeing USA in Russia said, I beg to disagree with my friend. He said the market in China for aircraft is seven times bigger. He said let me tell you why we're here. Russia has the best engineers in the world. Russia has intellectual capital. Russia is a great nation. Your titanium lets the planes fly that you buy.

PRIME MINISTER PUTIN: (As translated.) Allow me to make a point, we have the largest in the world engineering center here in Moscow.

VICE PRESIDENT BIDEN: There's a reason. Mr. Prime Minister, I've been around a long time. The first time I was here -- the second time I was here, I was here meeting with President Brezhnev. We were trying to pass SALT II --

END

12:58 P.M. (Local)

As you might imagine, the Vice President's staffers were furious with the Russians. I was instructed to have the transcript reflect how the Vice President had been cut off in mid sentence. So I sent them a transcript with the parenthetical phrase (Interruption to proceedings) as the closing. But they later decided to remove the parenthetical and just have the ending unexplained. That's how it is on the website to this day.

Joe Biden, for his part, worked diligently to promote several Putin requests. Days after getting bitch-slapped, Joe published an op-ed in the **International Herald Tribune** titled: *"The Next Steps in the U.S.-Russia Reset,"[11]* which in the hindsight of Putin's later aggressions towards our country and others appears almost criminally naive.

And then when Russia was accepted into the *World Trade Organization* in December 2011, and officially joined in August 2012, both Biden and Obama lauded Russia's "role" in world affairs.

Note the timing of when Putin got the highly publicized WTO win,

August 2012, just in time for Team Obama to use it against Romney-Ryan.

It saddens me to recall the mockery that Joe Biden and Barack Obama and their supporters directed against Mitt Romney for saying in an interview with Wolf Blitzer on CNN that Russia was "our number one geopolitical foe".[12]

Here's Joe having some fun at a speech in New York about a year after he was gonged in Moscow, again quoted from the transcript I prepared of that event.

> *"But just a month ago, Governor Romney called — and here again I quote, 'without question our number one geopolitical foe' is Russia. (Laughter.) As my brother would say, go figure. (Laughter.) And sometimes — I don't know whether it's a slip of the tongue or it's a mindset — but he refers to Russians as 'Soviets' — (laughter) — which I think — no, I think reveals a mindset."* [13]

The entire Democratic Party treated it as a big, funny joke. Time and time again I listened as audiences laughed heartily at Joe and Barack's witty put-downs of Mitt Romney's suspicions of Putin.

But those audiences hadn't seen Vladimir Putin bitch-slap Joe Biden like I had. I never laughed. The older you get political lies just stop being humorous.

Years later, after the truth of Team Obama's Russian "reset" was revealed through Putin's annexation of Crimea, Obama led the charge to eject Russia from the G8, thus deflecting the accusations of abject failure. But only deflecting.

Do any Democrats out there think Putin was honoring the spirit of the reset when the Russians hacked the State Department and White House unclassified email systems in November 2014? How about when the Russians went after our 2016 election process?

From what I had seen, the Russian reset was fake diplomacy, nothing less than Team Obama overhyped subterfuge, and it was a big reason why I knew Hillary Clinton would never win the presidency.

So, Joe, if you're going to sell your foreign policy credentials to be the next president of the United States, *don't use the Russian reset as a reference.*

A Point of Personal Privilege

CHAPTER FOUR

When your job is to record every public statement the Vice President of the United States makes, and you wind up not being able to do that because some pissed off Chinese guys are shoving you out of the room as he's speaking, like with all their strength shoving, like rugby scrum shoving, and they're wearing suits and ties, and you're wearing a suit and tie, and you're in the Great Hall of the People in Beijing, China, and the vice president you're working for is Joe Biden, who is oblivious to the mayhem being directed at you and others in the press pool covering him because he's rambling on and on about his personal privilege, you might think something *is amiss.*

The shoving stops. You compose yourself, straighten your tie, and realize incredulously that everyone in the room *except Joe Biden* understands he's just been humiliated.

And since it's the second time in your six months working for Vice President Joe Biden that his personal history ramblings have prompted his authoritarian hosts to publicly humiliate him, you start questioning if he knows what he's doing.

I sure was.

And then I started praying for a long healthy life for President Obama.

We were in China to advance President Obama's 2011-12 "Asia Pivot" —
his diplomatic effort that viewed the world's most populous country as
a rising economic rival in spite of a boatload of human rights issues; a
whopping trade imbalance with the United States; and dastardly business
practices.

This is how Team Obama looked upon China at the time.

Joe Biden's itinerary for our trip was two days in Beijing for meetings
with Chinese leaders, an American-Chinese business roundtable, a visit
to a noodle shop, and then a day out in the countryside near Chengdu,
a city of 10 million in giant panda territory. This beautiful area was near
the Himalayas, but there was no time to sight-see, as then we were back
in the air, off to Mongolia for a day, then onto Japan for two more.

The shoving episode, which came right at the beginning of the trip,
caught everyone by surprise. Though our pre-trip brief had advised
security awareness, especially with sensitive information, there was no
anticipation of menace like the Moscow trip. At this time China wasn't
viewed as aggressive, at least by the Obama White House, so our guard
was down.

Then came the shoving.

The first bout was aimed at the press pool group, which consisted of two
D.C.-based correspondents — Jeff Mason, of Reuters, and Mike Memoli,
then of *The Chicago Tribune,* a few local correspondents, plus a couple of
White House staffers.

They were standing quietly in an observation area, behind a rope and
stanchion barrier about 25 yards from where Vice President Joe Biden
and his delegation were meeting with then Vice President of China Xi

Jinping and his delegation. I was stationed beneath a loudspeaker in a different part of the room.

The press pool folks were doing as they were instructed: respectfully and professionally following the rules the Chinese laid down.

And then without warning, two plainclothes, male Chinese security agents walked up and assaulted them, pushing them roughly towards the exit.

Our press poolers objected, then physically pushed back against the Chinese aggressors, but they were no match under those shocking circumstances, especially since there was no reason for this sudden, baffling abuse.

And wouldn't you know, as all this is taking place, Joe Biden is still prattling on to Xi Jinping who is staring back at him in that frozen-face, Chinese leader kind of way that enables them to deploy their goons without so much as wrinkling a brow.

Interesting, too, that the goons started shoving just when Joe started geezing about his personal legacy.

Long, boring, self-aggrandizing speeches don't play well with authoritarian leaders. Not that Joe Biden has to kowtow to the Xis and the Putins of the world, but as we saw in Moscow and now in China, his rambling egoism gave them an opening to embarrass him right to his face.

The lesson: Chinese leaders decide what people beneath them deserve, they enforce those decisions with violence, and everybody is beneath them — including Americans representing the White House.

And the Vice President came off, predictably, as weak.

World leaders with less nerve put up with the long speeches, as do star-struck Americans and fawning media. But people who know Joe and listen to him a lot, especially his staffers, steel themselves for the inevitable "point of personal privilege" monologues.

Joe Biden's bloviating about his early days in Russia had cued up Putin's put-down, and then when Joe did it again with his stone-faced Chinese hosts, the scene of humiliation was repeated.

> *"As we say in the chamber where I worked for 36 years, the United States Senate", he intoned before the Chinese, "if you permit me a point of personal privilege"* —

That's all it took — WHAM — the shoving started. Joe Biden, God love him, is Joe Biden, *and so he just kept on talking.*

Where I was beneath the loudspeaker watching the spectacle from across the room, I saw them finish abusing the press pool and shove them out the room, and then they came for me. I struggled and held them off a minute, but only that.

The attack on me effectively ceased my ability to record and do my job. The interrupted transcript I later produced, still visible on the Obama White House website, concludes with a special parenthetical note — "(End of recording)" — Showing how that the recording was stopped before Joe actually concluded his remarks.

The White House
Office of the Vice President
For Immediate Release
August 18, 2011

Remarks by Vice President Biden

in a Meeting with Chinese Vice President XI

The Great Hall of the People

Beijing, China

10:40 A.M. (Local)

VICE PRESIDENT XI: Honorable, Mr. Vice President, Joseph Biden, the ancient Chinese philosopher Confucius said, isn't it delightful to welcome friends coming from afar? I would like to, again, extend a warm welcome to you.

Your visit this time is a major event in this year's China-U.S. relationship, and it's very important for further implementing the outcomes of President Hu Jintao's visit to the United States, and to pushing forward the building of the China-U.S. cooperative partnership.

Mr. Vice President, you've been in China twice. You've long cared about and been committed to promoting the China-U.S. relationship. Your belief that a successful, stable and prosperous China is good for the United States and, of course, for China and good for the whole world. I appreciate that statement.

I, too, believe that under the new situation China and the United States have evermore extensive common interests, and we shoulder evermore important common responsibilities. It is the joint desire of the people of China and the United States and elsewhere in the world to see a close cooperation between China and the United States. We would like to work with your country to promote the development of relations between our two great nations.

Our talks this morning is an important component of your engagements and activities here. I would like to have an in-depth exchange of views with you on our bilateral relationship and international and regional issues of mutual interest.

VICE PRESIDENT BIDEN: Mr. Vice President, and, delegations, it's a genuine honor to be here. It's an honor to be back in China. As you know, as you mentioned, Mr. Vice President, this is -- it's been 10 years since I've been here last. And my first visit was in 1979 when I had the honor of being with Vice Premier Deng Xiaoping at the time.

I've always been an admirer of the Chinese people and the great sweep of history and the contributions that your country has made for centuries. When I arrived in 1979, I got the first opportunity I ever had to see some of the great wonders of this country, including as all visitors mention, I'm sure, the Great Wall. But I would presume to suggest that in the great sweep of your history, there has been more progress made between 1979 and 2011 than maybe any time in your history. It's amazing. You personally and all your colleagues should be complimented.

I come from the United States, Mr. Vice President, at the invitation of your President and you with hope and expectation and looking forward to your reciprocal visit to Washington.

I also come with a strong message that the United States of America is -- plans on looking -- will continue to be engaged totally in the world and events of the world; and maybe even a stronger message that our commitment to establish a close and serious relationship with the people of China is of the utmost importance to my country and -- presumptuous of me to say -- I think maybe your country, as well.

Fifty years from now, 100 years from now, historians and scholars will judge us based upon whether or not we're able to establish a strong, permanent and friendly working relationship.

For I would suggest that there's no more important relationship that we need to establish on the part of the United States than a close relationship with China.

As we say in the chamber where I worked for 36 years, the United States Senate, if you permit me a point of personal privilege: I came away from our visit in Rome greatly impressed -- impressed with your sweep and knowledge of history, impressed with your openness and candor and impressed with the notion that you, as I -- and I know your ambassador believes -- that foreign policy is more than just formal visits; it's establishing personal relationships and trust. And it is my fond hope that our personal relationship will continue to grow, as well.

Let me conclude by saying to you and your colleagues, Mr. Vice President, that I'm absolutely confident that the economic stability of the world rests in no small part on the cooperation between -- between the United States and China. It affects every country from your neighbor to the north, to Argentina in the southern tip of South America. It is the key, in my view, to global economic stability.

(End of recording.) [14]

END

10:51 A.M. (Local)

The Chinese did eventually fess up. Their reasoning was, by my thinking, outlandish, but then I didn't grow up in the surveillance and control society that is the People's Republic of China.

Essentially, the Chinese declared Joe Biden a boorish blabbermouth. One of their officials, a young woman, explained to the press pool that while then-Vice President Xi spoke for only two and a half minutes, Vice President Biden *spoke for much longer.* Her demeanor made it clear that, *of course, this affront meant they could physically assault staffers and press.*

Close reading of the transcript bears the Chinese out. Xi delivered his remarks for about three of the eleven minutes both men were talking, which means Biden was hogging the floor for about three times as long as his host. And that doesn't account for the time he spoke after my recorder was forced off.

But the Chinese reasoning doesn't explain why the Vice President was passive while it was happening, and why he simply kept talking.

Talk about a point of personal privilege.

Thanks to our two pool reporters filing notes on the shoving, though, at least this revealing and embarrassing exhibition was amplified beyond the pool report into the broader media. A few outlets published tidbits on it.

The pro-Obama magazine, *The Atlantic,* referred to it as "bizarre". Mike Memoli wrote a blow-by-blow account for his *Chicago Tribune's* affiliate, *The Los Angeles Times,* and his pool report was quoted in *The New Yorker* magazine.

Obviously, these are odd outcomes for a vice president who has bragged incessantly about his vast experience in foreign affairs.

You see, this was not the first time I'd been in that elegant room in the Great Hall of the People. I'd gone there with Vice President Cheney in 2004. When he made his remarks in meetings with the Chinese, there was no shoving. There was no need for it. Cheney's remarks were succinct and respectful of Chinese sensibilities.

Unlike Joe Biden, Dick Cheney did not to promote himself at the expense of his president's or his country's objectives.

But apparently the Chinese, just like Putin, knew Joe Biden's weakness.

Nor were they done pushing back.

During a later meeting with chair of the National People's Congress, Wu Bangguo, Joe went slightly beyond his "time limit", so the Chinese, of course, countered with a wall-to-wall line of marching security agents who cleared the press from the room well before the Vice President had finished his statement.

No shoving this time, but an overwhelming show of force, which Joe Biden tried in vain to talk over. Not sure why. My guess is he wanted to appear powerful in front of his Chinese hosts, though clearly their intended message was that he was not.

I remember looking back at him as he watched me and the other press poolers being forced from the room. I kept recording, even after I turned for the exit, I had the microphone pointed at him over my shoulder as I was ushered to the door, but it was futile. The recorder playback was of Joe Biden's indiscernible remarks and the tight-lipped rustlings of an authoritarian regime's robotic heavies.

Joe saw what was happening, and he just kept at it — talking to a room of people who could care less what he said. I can't imagine what he was thinking, but I'd bet it wasn't: *Wow, this is going well.*

But then Joe seemed to catch on. The next few times he spoke publicly with Chinese leaders, he stayed obediently within their unofficial time limits.

In my years of White House travel, I've found China to be a hurly burly place for Western journalists, including me when I'm in the press pool. They are far more physically disrespectful of journalists than European, African, South American, or other Asian countries. But having such a public show of disrespect for the vice president of the United States was unprecedented. In my mind, Obama's Asia Pivot, with Joe Biden as its spokesman, was getting off to a rough start with the Chinese.

Joe, though, does not give up easily. Obama's affable vice president cranked up the charm and the Chinese seemed to buy it. The rest of the trip went well, with Biden and Xi spending a lot of time together in Chengdu.

And to his credit, Joe scored some points on the Chinese on that trip. He gave them a dire assessment of the impending social disaster of their one-child policy, which they soon amended.

Definitely a win for Joe, Team Obama, and Chinese families.

And he straightened out the Chinese when they started kvetching about the far-fetched possibility of the U.S. defaulting on our debt obligations, as if we were Russia or some such nonsense.

As I write this in winter 2020 watching the campaigns for the November presidential elections underway, Joe is still out there selling his "personal relationship" with President Xi.

But my question is: Joe, who benefited from that "personal relationship"? Everyday Americans? Or only Team Obama, Joe Biden and his family members, and the Chinese leadership?

In 2011-2012, as the media had it, President Obama and his team were at the top of their game, with Joe Biden as one of their leading scorers. Old pol that he is, he knew just how to broaden his efforts for the team into a "personal privilege". His efforts for the Asia Pivot reflected that.

Upon return from that trip, he won the high profile role of being Team Obama's point man on China. A cozy relationship with Xi promised the foreign policy wins Team Obama wanted for their re-election highlight reel. Joe was their man.

There was talk about cooperation on climate change. There was talk about cooperation on trade. There was talk about cooperation on international security. The media obediently ate it up, just as they ate up the Russian reset.

Talk, talk, lots of talk.

And then, thanks to Joe, a bit later back in America, there was an actual China-USA deal, and if you lived around Hollywood, it was a very big deal indeed.

Don't ever underestimate Joe Biden. Beneath his "kid from Scranton" schtick, there is a crafty politician who can play his "point of personal privilege" to the utmost. In the past, that image could only take him so far. Joe's previous presidential campaign flame-outs (1988 and 2008) had taught him that he sorely lacked two key elements to win in the critical

Iowa caucus: gobs of money and media attention. But now Team Obama was going to build something new for the 2012 re-election cycle, and the Vice President was going to play an important role in making it happen.

In other words, for the re-election fight against Mitt Romney and for his own future presidential ambitions later, Joe Biden and Team Obama needed a killer strategy. After preparing first in China, it was now time for *Joey goes to Hollywood.*

A Point of Personal Privilege:
Joey Goes to Hollywood

CHAPTER FIVE

Afew months after our Chegdu trip, Joe Biden shrewdly leveraged his blossoming relationship with Xi. In the process the Vice President developed serious new Hollywood pals, and this paid off with lucrative fund-raising events. Talk about a win-win.

Joe made this all happen by personally escorting Xi to high-profile Los Angeles meetings beginning in February 2012. Hollywood movers and shakers vied for their attention, which Joe meted out judiciously.

Why would Xi Jinping want to spend time in Hollywood? China is a massive market for American filmmakers, but at that time Chinese leaders were severely restricting the number of American films allowed into their theaters. Hollywood wanted more access to this booming market and China wanted better control over how the country and its government was presented throughout the entertainment world.

So Joe, with the help of his old friend Chris Dodd, former Democratic senator from Connecticut, and coincidentally the chief lobbyist for the motion picture industry, the Vice President stuck in his thumb and pulled out a plum.

Team Obama began by setting up cross-country trip for Xi, including a two-day bonanza of Los Angeles events featuring Xi and Biden in tandem meeting important Hollywood producers and filmmakers. Soon a new deal was sealed so U.S. studios could distribute more films into China and, as well, increase their box office share.

Opening up the restricted Chinese market was a big win for the studios, for California, and for motion picture industry jobs, and for the Joe Biden cadre in Team Obama.

From the outset of his campaign in 2008, Hollywood donors had lavished Obama with stacks of cash and star-power attention. Joe's link with Xi and his helping hand had now paid them back handsomely.

For years to come, whenever he spoke in front of campaign rallies, and especially donor gatherings, Joe Biden would wax eloquent about his personal relationship with Xi, who would eventually move into the presidency of China in 2013, and later ordain himself "president for life" in 2018.

I guarantee Joe thinks his "personal" relationship with Xi is a privileged feather in his cap that sets him apart from the other Democratic presidential candidates for the 2020 race.

But the real question is whether Joe's special relationship been good for America? Or just China?

Here's a Joe Biden pearl of wisdom from an op-ed he wrote for *The New York Times* shortly after returning from our trip in 2011. In my opinion, this is Joe Biden articulating what Team Obama thought was a workable approach to China. Every word in this sentence screams "soft power", with the emphasis on soft. Joe wrote:

> "We are clear-eyed about concerns like China's growing military

abilities and intentions; that is why we are engaging with the Chinese military to understand and shape their thinking."

Shape their thinking? Really? Is Joe Biden going to campaign for president on his ability to "shape" China's thinking?

Just look at the severe hardships the Chinese government is imposing on their citizens during the horrific Coronavirus outbreak in Wuhan. Brutality and intimidation seem to be their go-to philosophy.

Nothing Joe Biden ever said or did in regards to China has had anywhere near the impact as President Trump's trade talks/tariffs toughness.

You want to "shape" the thinking of Chinese leadership, follow Trump's example and strip the artifice out of their parasitic economy. That will take it down a few notches.

Add Trump's unrivaled pressure on North Korea and you see his big thinking.

But it was the second time I worked for Joe Biden on a trip to China that I got a much better sense of his "point of personal privilege" attitude because on that trip, in December 2013, his son Hunter was on the plane, as well.

This trip started in Japan and included stops in China, before concluding in South Korea with a brief visit to the DMZ for a "stare-down" photo-op directed toward the North Koreans from the safety of sandbagged observation post.

(Contrast that to President Trump's stroll into the DMZ to actually shake Kim Jong Un's hand.)

Besides Hunter Biden's freeloading on his dad's trip to set up a business deal, the unreported story on that 2013 China trip was Joe's backing off from an "up yours" Air Force Two flight.

China at the time was provocatively expanding its maritime presence in the South China Sea. Then it took the outrageous step of declaring an air travel security zone well beyond its borders and insisted it would defend it with military action.

Remember what I said about Chinese leaders and violence?

Well, on the flight from Japan into China, the rumor spread around the plane that we were to broach their ridiculous air travel security zone by flying Air Force Two right through it on the way to Beijing. Staffers were fired up. This was just the kind of big symbolic statement Joe loved.

But then nothing came of it. We flew into Beijing without incident on a standard flight path. No symbolic broach, no grand gesture.

It was all talk, just talk.

The Chinese were less contentious on this visit than in 2011, but that didn't mean they were welcoming hosts.

After one event, the press pool journalists went to the U.S. embassy to file their stories (transcripts in my case) and couldn't get through to the internet in what was supposed to be a secure environment. Turns out the Chinese had shut down the embassy's primary internet access (embassy staffers indicated it happens quite frequently). So all of us scrambled up portable wi-fi to meet our deadlines.

There's that lesson again: Chinese leaders decide what people beneath them deserve, they enforce those decisions with violence, and everybody is beneath them — including Americans representing the White House.

But now there's a bigger story of that 2013 trip, as reported in Peter Schweizer's book and Adam Entous' article in the *New Yorker* magazine, that Hunter Biden just happened to bump into some Chinese business partners who later agreed to a lucrative deal.

The allegation is that Hunter used his father's position to advance his business interests — both Vice President Biden and Hunter Biden deny this, but the investigation is underway.

I recall Hunter being on the plane with his daughter, Finnegan, the second eldest of his three daughters, but I never saw them. They mostly kept separate schedules from the vice president's official duties, which is typical for when family members came along.

And that just demonstrates how easy it was for Hunter Biden to do his Chinese business while the focus was on his father.

There were good reporters in the pool on that trip — Josh Feldman, with the Associated Press wire service; David Nakamura, with *The Washington Post*; Mark Landler, with *The New York Times;* and Steve Clemons, with *The Atlantic* magazine. But their job was to observe and report on Joe.

And though Joe Biden often took his second wife, Jill, their grandkids, and occasionally his daughters-in-law on overseas trips with him, this was the only time I traveled overseas with either of his sons. So this was not just a sightseeing trip for Hunter.

Nor do I have anything to add to what has already been excellent reporting about Hunter Biden's business dealings in China.

But then it wasn't just China, was it? Hunter Biden was after it in Ukraine, as well.

Given Adam Entous' reporting on what Hunter Biden, then in the throes of his addiction, was doing to himself and his family, I don't think his dad knew what to do about his son.

I don't judge the Bidens. Addiction is a horrible burden to live with, and hiding it is part of the pathology. Hunter and his dad are not unlike like a lot of fathers and sons, the world over.

As a matter of fact, I have always admired Joe Biden's lifelong abstinence from drugs and alcohol (and Donald Trump's). He and President Trump both found their answer to a hallmark human frailty and lived it daily. Their bravery has my respect.

But addiction does not excuse poor judgment and extreme carelessness — by either father or son. Maybe Hunter Biden will eventually offer more clarity about his father's knowledge of his business dealings in China and Ukraine. Maybe not. He's in recovery, and I wish him the best.

But without a doubt what I do see is a privileged carelessness, if not deceptively by the father, then recklessly by the son.

And where do careless "point of personal privilege" sons learn their life lessons? From their careless "point of personal privilege" dads.

Hollywood, Gays and Guns

CHAPTER SIX

There is genius in Joe Biden.

But he's so good at camouflaging it, you won't see it unless you know where to look.

Fresh from his movie deal success with Xi Jinping, Joe Biden, in April 2012, returned to Hollywood for an informal talk at a fundraiser in a private home and effortlessly accomplished what I rate as one of the high points of his career, if not his life. I wasn't invited, but I listened in.

Unforgettably, I might add.

President Obama spoke about hope and change for eight years. But for all the talk, there was only one instance I saw of actual hope and change of the kind Obama worshippers dreamed of, and it was Joe Biden who pulled it off.

And what did our vice president do? Simple, really: He offered an honest heartfelt response to an honest heartfelt question.

But given the man he was, the office he held, the political era he inhabited, it was Joe Biden's answer that uncorked America's acceptance of same-sex marriage and forever raised the trajectory of our society to a higher and better plane.

Hopefully someday that acceptance will be global.

Let's not kid ourselves, Joe's intention at that April 2012 Hollywood event was to raise money, not the human condition.

But while there, in the middle of a predictable evening of raising funds, he recognized a moment of extraordinary political opportunity where no one else did. That is the genius of Joe. He didn't get himself into the vice presidency without it.

It was a celebrity fundraiser that followed the script that most White House fundraisers do: Gravitas grubbing for cash. Impress the hell out of some very hard to impress people and pass the hat.

Joe Biden knew the drill by heart. His motorcade would roll into an opulent private residence. Donors waiting inside would hear the roar of his police escort motorcycles. They would see a procession of powerful government vehicles all deferring to Joe's shiny black SUV with blue and white Office of Vice President flags flapping smartly on the front hood.

Upon arrival, Joe's Secret Service detail would swarm the house — watchful, lethal agents talking discreetly into their sleeves. Respectful of the residence, respectful of the donors — impressive men and women, trustworthy protectors of the vice president, and yes, they were there for the guests' protection too.

Special times.

Then Joe would bound into the room — aviator sunglasses, dazzling toothy smile, folksy greeting at the ready: *"hey, man!"*

He'd shake hands, slap backs, grab shoulders, arms. Spontaneous hugs. It's his "Joe of the people" thing, in which he treated the crowd as all equally worthy of his embrace, male and female, whether he was with Hollywood movers and shakers, like this time, or at other events where he was dealing with "average people", he was the same Joe Biden, on a mission to make contact. I always saw his behavior in these close quarters as chummy, not creepy. But you see what you look for.

At these kinds of meetings, after a bit of glad handing, Joe would say a few words about how he and Barack appreciated the support so they could carry on fighting the good fight. He'd drop a couple of jokes about dopey Republicans, and considering the special location this time, hopefully (for his future presidential aspirations) nail down some good Hollywood contacts.

And that's basically what happened at this particular fundraiser until suddenly near the end when Joe Biden made *"hope and history rhyme"*.

(That's a line from a poem Joe loves, *"The Cure at Troy"*, by Seamus Heaney. Joe adores his Irish poets, though it is a bunglefest every time he attempts to quote them.)

One of the best (and worst) aspects of my job is when I hear something significant, it stays in my memory — endlessly. Because speech and sound stir our emotions deeply into our memories. Politicians know this. Musicians know this. Actors know this. Hollywood knows this.

And where was I while Joe Biden's history-making words were being voiced? I was listening to it all, sitting alone in my office in Washington, D.C., connected to this Hollywood reception by a special White House Communications Agency (WHCA) live transmission. The audio was being sent specifically to me for immediate transcription.

Despite this cross-country link-up, only I and the attendees could hear the proceedings. And that was it, no one outside of that room heard it. Nothing of that gathering was ever broadcast publicly or shared with the public.

Though a fundraiser, this was a closed press event with no working media present (it was Hollywood, so, of course, media were there as donors). But no public reporting on what was said was allowed. That leaves my transcript and the WHCA recording (both available post-2022 through FOIA requests) as the only official record.

And since neither of these records were later distributed to the press, this event was all behind the scenes.

That's standard procedure for fundraising events. It's rare for the press to be allowed in. First of all, they'd scarf the hors d'oeuvres, then they'd write something snarky about the principal, or worse, the donors. So barring the press from fundraisers is standard for both parties.

At this event, after his opening remarks, Joe opened the floor to questions. My recollection is that there were a couple of thoughtful policy questions and then someone, possibly Joe himself, invited one of the hosts, a gay man, to ask a question.

And this gay gentleman, whom I never saw but clearly and unforgettably heard, asked Joe something to the effect of: How do you feel about us? Really, how do you feel about *us?*

And from 3,000 miles away I could hear the intensity in that room as everyone there collectively hushed into the moment.

Not because they were extra polite but because they smelled history.

They knew that host. He was their friend. They accepted his invitation to affirm him and the politics they all shared.

And what everyone there knew was that host, that successful gay man who lived lovingly in Barack Obama's America with his partner and their children, was essentially asking the question gay men and lesbian women had borne in silence and near isolation for centuries: *How do you feel about us? Really, how do you feel about us?*

And what struck me and probably Joe Biden was the tone in which the gentleman asked the question.

It was tremulous. That's the only way I can describe it — tremulous, as though meting out an equal measure of fear and hope — fear of the disapproval that LGBTQ folks had always faced with that question and hope that maybe — just maybe — this time the disapproval would vanish.

As is their practice when they sent me audio of vice presidential events, the good professionals at WHCA archived it. Hopefully, someday, someone will find it and share it with the public, because *it is historic.*

There was definitely *hope* in that question. For the first time in history, this gentleman was in a position to get a face-to-face answer from a White House that had seriously promised but not yet delivered unequivocal support for gay marriage. So what did Barack Obama's progressive White House really feel about them, the gay and lesbian Americans who helped elect them?

And while in retrospect it now seems obvious, at that point in time it wasn't. Not even close.

Because, remember, I didn't just work for Joe; I worked for President Obama, too.

Months prior to Joe's Hollywood fundraiser, back in December 2010, I was sitting in a chair along the back wall of the Oval Office when Barack Obama told an earnest and intelligent woman who reported for *The Advocate,* a website that covered LGBTQ issues, that his attitudes on gay marriage (that's what they called it back then) were "evolving".

I will never forget the tone in that conversation, either. As I recall, President Obama spoke with the deepest caution, delivering his answer with such word-by-word hesitation, it was almost as if he was dismantling the verbal equivalent of an unexploded bomb.

No doubt all the heckling he had been receiving from gay rights activists in the previous months had him on high alert.

Then after the reporter, Kerry Eleveld, who pushed Obama hard in her interview, was long gone, and I was waiting outside the Oval Office for an escort, I remember President Obama appearing in the reception area to complain loudly to his staffers, *"I can't get no love",* as though he was doing so much and still not being fully appreciated.

Or maybe fully adored.

And while *The Advocate* released their transcript of that interview, the White House transcript was not released to the public.

Up until Joe Biden's intervention, "evolving" was the best Barack Obama could offer LGTBQ Americans.

And so back to our Hollywood host, and his plaintive question, *"how do you feel about us"* — well, fortunately for that gentleman and American history, he got Joe Biden at his best. And then, because he was the vice president of the United States who deeply desired to be THE president, so did we all.

The world over.

That question and the gentleman's tremulous delivery of it struck the tuning fork of Joe's political soul and his instinctive response brought our country one giant leap closer to a more perfect union.

Joe Biden, vice president of the United States, looked at the man's children, who were gathered with him and his partner, and he spoke father-to-father, man-to-man, respect-to-respect saying, from the transcript I prepared, *"What did I do when I walked in?"*

The host replied, *"You walked right to my children. They were seven and five, giving you flowers."*

Now comes the genius of Joe. He simply told the gathering the truth of that family he saw sitting right in front of him, *"I wish every American could see the look of love those kids had in their eyes for you guys. And they wouldn't have any doubt about what this is about."*

In that simple, heartfelt answer, Joe Biden brought not only that room together, but as the vice president, his words represented the whole country coming together behind the truth that a family is people who love and protect each other, and loving families are the bedrock of civilization. This is something I think we can all agree on.

I do. LGBTQ folks are my family and friends, work colleagues and respected public figures. I love them and I love their families. We are all in this together.

And then after speaking his truth, Joe said his goodbyes and zoomed off to Washington where he put his thumbprint on American history.

That occurred about one week later during an interview with David

Gregory on NBC's *"Meet the Press"*, when Joe said publicly in front of a national television audience, *"Look, I am vice president of the United States of America. The president sets the policy. I am absolutely comfortable with the fact that men marrying men, women marrying women, and heterosexual men and women marrying one another are entitled to the same exact rights — all the civil rights, all the civil liberties. And quite frankly, I don't see much of a distinction beyond that."*

As for the transcripts of that bold statement, the one I prepared was not publicly released, though the NBC *"Meet the Press"* transcript is viewable on their website.

It's important to understand Joe did not have clearance to publicly express himself on gay marriage like that. He was way out ahead of Team Obama on live national television on that.

Wow.

And you know it's a big deal if Joe Biden's blunt honesty forces *the whole of Barack Obama's White House* to agree with him.

David Axelrod, Valerie Jarrett and others were livid. Barack Obama not so much. This may have been the beginning — for better or worse — of him trusting Joe to be his wingman.

So credit Joe Biden for flinging out into the political firmament the heartfelt answer to a heartfelt question so many politicians — Democrats and Republicans— had feared for so long.

That brave gay father, on behalf of his children, was the voice of hope, and Joe Biden was the voice of change — real change — for the betterment of our entire country. We owe Joe for that.

So thank you, Mr. Vice President. Your words "freed a lot of souls", and it was my honor to hear you speak them and type them into history.

If the story ended there, we'd have a happy Hollywood ending. But this is real life, so it doesn't.

As much as Joe is willing to speak an amazing truth when it matters (and feeds his ambition), he's also willing to stay amazingly silent when it matters (and threatens his ambition).

But there is an important irony to recognize as our nation grapples with our scourge of mass shootings. I will say unequivocally that Joe Biden and his Democratic Party have stayed far too silent for far too long on one of its causes: the entertainment industry's unrestricted marketing of violent content to our children.

This would be the very same Hollywood that Joe and Barack relied upon for their fundraising and star-powered media messaging.

Not a coincidence.

In response to the wrenching tragedy of the Newtown shooting in December 2012, President Obama declared his intention to "fix" our gun laws.

As I wrote in my book *Fifteen Years A Deplorable: A White House Memoir,* he should never have politicized that tragedy as he did.

Our country's emotions around it were so raw, and Barack Obama's decision to use it as leverage against the Republican Party and the NRA was an epic fail with the self-destructive outcome that both sides of the electorate became certain of the other's inherent evil.

No longer was the other party simply flawed in their thinking, but they were morally destitute. Democrats thought that of Republicans, and Republicans thought that of Democrats.

This political combat was scorched earth politics, and there are no winners in scorched earth politics. There are no ties in scorched earth politics. *Everyone loses.*

Thus the political divisions in our country grew darker and deeper in hatred and incivility as accusation and counter-accusation grew harsher.

But that was Barack Obama's decision to lead in that direction, and to accomplish it, he put Joe Biden in charge.

Joe Biden seemed the logical choice for a second run at a restrictive firearms policy. He was the author of the original, and largely ineffective "assault weapons ban" for the Democrats in 1994, which the Bush administration had allowed to sunset in 2004.

The problem was that Team Obama's approach of blaming gun owners, gun manufacturers, and the National Rifle Association for the horrific tragedy at Newtown was as flawed as it was divisive. The accusations did not address Hollywood's dirty and lucrative business of marketing ever more obnoxious, sexualized, and violent video games, movies and TV shows to our children.

We are dehumanizing our children. We are progressively dehumanizing the childhood of our nation's next generation. All of us.

They are selling deviant human behavior cheap and at scale, and we are allowing our children to become its addicts.

I define "we" as the adults who permit our children unrestricted access to dehumanizing content, and "they" are the Hollywood creators selling it to them year by year as the children grow into their adulthood.

If we are all in this together to promote the good, we should all be in this together to eradicate the bad.

Right, Hollywood?

There is not much in our amazing world that I hate, but I do hate certain words — namely hypocrisy and demagoguery. Unfortunately, they underpin every White House discussion of mass shootings I've ever heard. From both the Democrats and the Republicans.

Both.

But each side, especially those at the furthest end of the spectrum, sees only the hypocrisy of the other, never their own

America is flooded with guns. There are more guns in our country than ever in our history — though probably not per capita. Extremely conservative estimates put that number at over 200 million.

A lot of those guns — again, a conservative estimate is 30 percent — are semi-automatic handguns bought and owned legally by responsible owners. A much smaller percentage of those guns are semi-automatic rifles, what some people refer to as "assault rifles".

The vast majority of those guns are never used in a crime or act of violence. But it only takes one semi-automatic rifle in the wrong hands to generate headlines (and media attention) for weeks.

Yet there are LESS gun-related murders per capita being committed in America's major cities (with the exception of Chicago and Baltimore and a couple others) at this time in our history than there has been for decades.

More guns, less gun murders, per capita.

That's great news except gun death rates — often redefined as gun violence — are again on the rise, but not solely because of murders.

Joe Biden will tell you, as he discussed regularly and publicly during his gun violence task force from 2013 through 2014, that the majority of gun deaths in America are suicide-related.

In 2010, of the roughly 31,00 deaths from guns, two-thirds were from suicides. In 2017, of the almost 40,000 deaths from guns, two-thirds were from suicides, according to Pew Research figures.

It has to be said, too, that in this era of increasingly violent content, solo gun suicides are becoming less a solo tragedy.

The tragic news that entire families are being murdered by a suicidal parent or child (and not always with guns) is, in my opinion, more prevalent now than ever in American history. Most American mass shooters are on, more often than not, a rage-fueled quest for violence that ends in suicide.

Why are Americans filled with rage? Why are Americans seeing their lives as unlivable? Why are Americans seeing their families as disposable? Why are Americans mass murdering their fellow human beings? What corruption guides their mind and their heart into this sort of atrocity?

The answer, in my opinion, is because somewhere along the way these poor souls lost their humanity. And then our Hollywood-fueled, American gun culture reinforces their rage to the point of public tragedy.

There are deranged Americans among us who see their fellow citizens gathered in a place of worship, or a place of business, or a school, or a festival, or a nightclub as targets.

Not human beings, targets.

Like they see in a video game. Or a zombie apocalypse movie.

And here's the Hollywood/media hypocrisy part. We see nightly newscasts on every major broadcast network of reporters and anchors saddened, concerned, bewildered by the murderous headlines they report of shootings and gun atrocities. But then, within minutes of the end of their news report, these same networks broadcast a crime drama chock full of shootings and gun atrocities.

Every major network does this and has for decades. So aren't the networks through their news reporters' airing of stories on gun violence also simultaneously promoting their crime dramas that feature fictional gun violence?

Sure seems that way to me. What about you?

Nor is it a coincidence that the guns used in real street crime are the same ones that Hollywood likes to depict most vividly in their violent content "creations".

Relentlessly effective advertising, product placement, impressions — Hollywood/Democrats, own your role in America's gun culture.

Joe Biden knows when Democrats rage at gun manufacturers without simultaneously raging at their most effective advertisers — Hollywood — they will never solve anything.

Pretty quiet on that, though, aren't you, Joe?

And the indoctrination is getting worse. There is more violent content on far more channels, websites, streaming services, cinemas, game consoles, et cetera, than ever in our history. It's not filtering into our society, it's addicting our society, and more than ever, our youth.

Recall the successful anti-tobacco campaign led by the Democrats. Joe Biden does. He was in on that.

I agree with anyone who says cigarette smoking is a self-destructive habit that is an expensive liability to our public health. The Democrats certainly said that. They were right to work to restrict our kids' exposure to it.

And who helped them do that? Who stopped filming movies and TV shows that were peopled with sophisticated heroes and heroines who smoked?

Hollywood.

But where are they on our kids' addiction to violent content?

Pushing it.

Joe understands Hollywood bears some responsibility for America's gun culture. He knew that during his gun violence task force effort but publicly said next to nothing about it.

And while he scheduled meetings with the NRA, gun manufacturers, and hunting groups, as well as executives from the video gaming industry and the movie industry, when it came time to roll out Team Obama's plan, he let the Democrats' golden ticket donors off the hook and went after gun owners.

Never, not once did he come out and publicly express his views on violent video games, television shows, or movies.

The closest he came to publicly airing his opinion was at a 2013 meeting with video game industry representatives that was videotaped by the White House and uploaded to YouTube.[15]

Vice President Biden hinted at his view by quoting Senator Daniel Patrick Moynihan's concept of *"defining deviancy down"* and then posing the question of what is responsible for *"the coarsening of our culture"*.

But that was it.

Hollywood got a backstage pass from first Joe, then President Obama while they spoke for the Democrats.

And all of America knows it. That's why gun control is so divisive. Because to solve it, our country has to be honest with itself.

I certainly heard Joe talk passionately about violent video game content in statements he made in private at fundraisers and closed press events several times.

I recall him speaking vehemently about the sickening violence in video games as being deeply disturbing to him.

And while I never heard him refer to video game industry representatives as *"scumbags"*, that is the term he used before their 2013 meeting, according to Kyle Orland's excellent reporting in *Ars **Technica.***

And in those instances when I heard him criticizing that industry, I made a transcript of it because that was my job. So it's in the official record somewhere, but, again, it won't be accessible until Obama administration records become publicly available in 2022.

Unless Joe wants to *now* speak that sentiment he so rightly spoke of then.

But I don't think he does.

Joe could be speaking the truth of that issue *now* and highlighting Hollywood's role in it as he campaigns for the presidency, but he won't. He can't.

Joe used to offer a poignant bit of advice for up and coming politicians who'd ask him the secret to winning. *"You have to know what it's worth losing over"*, he'd say.

What he means is if publicly holding a position on an issue that you know in your gut is elemental for you, to the point of being essential to your own personal humanity, but your voters will hate you for it, and publicly upholding it will cost you your election, do you state your position to please your voters or honor the integrity of your gut?

Clearly, on Hollywood's promoting gun violence, Joe Biden is choosing his politics over his humanity.

One thing I learned after working in the White House for a span of 15 years is that *"there are no guns there"*. Even though the place is chock full of heavy armament, semi-automatic rifles, and pistols, there are *"no guns"*.

But there are weapons and firearms.

Lots of them.

Every day at the White House, I saw weapons almost everywhere I turned. Hundreds of Secret Service agents and Uniformed Division Officers patrol the complex. All of them carry a semi-automatic pistol. You stop noticing after awhile.

But you never stop appreciating.

The most serious weapons are in strategic placements and expert hands.

Occasionally, I'd see the CAT Teamers, the snipers and heavy weapons guys, walking through the complex with their extra-large carry cases.

They're the ones who stand the critical watch. No matter the conditions — paralyzing cold, smothering heat, drenching rain, or blinding snow — every second of every day, they're out there protecting the People's House.

For all of us.

Whenever I could, I always held the door for them. My way of saying thanks.

I'm not sure the weapons and the professionals who bear them in protection of the White House ever made an appearance on the TV show *The West Wing,* but they should have. In the real world, they are as much a part of that place as the color of the paint.

And you can be sure there will never be the slightest restrictions on any weapons used to protect the White House. Or Hollywood luminaries. Or titans of industry.

So why then, with the rights of the Second Amendment, would everyday Americans be constitutionally restricted in any way from buying weapons of self-protection for their house? Or their family? Or their person?

Since the founding of this country, they never have.

And as Americans living under the protection of the Second Amendment of the Constitution, we get to decide what that protection means for us —

each of us, individually.

Of course, not every American owns a firearm. In fact, the majority do not. But not all of that majority are up in arms about Americans arming themselves.

A subset of the majority interprets their fellow Americans' desire for a weapon as a personal threat to them and their families. I believe this may be because they have absorbed so much Hollywood-produced violent content which feeds the emotions and fears wrapped around this issue.

But behind their fear lies the nagging truth that while the vast majority of firearm owners are law-abiding and responsible, some are not.

But what do we — all of us — do about that?

There have been a few gun incidents at the White House over the years, and since this is my memoir, I'll tell you about the one I almost stumbled into.

On Veterans Day evening 2011, a Friday, I walked from my office in the Eisenhower Executive Office Building to my vehicle parked on the Ellipse at about 8:30 p.m.

I was heading to a friend's 50th birthday party, so rather than my customary bus commute, I had driven in through D.C. traffic that day.

I passed by the guard shack at the Southwest Gate, waved good night, and got an agreeable nod from the Secret Service Uniform Division officers stationed there.

It was a short, carefree walk to my Xterra. All was in order. It was a quiet moment in a quiet place, end of a White House workweek. But by the time

I had driven the half-mile distance around the Ellipse to Constitution Avenue exit, everything had changed.

Though only five minutes had elapsed, since my cheery wave to the guards at the Southwest gate, I was inside a massive security response.

My exit was blocked by several Uniform Division cruisers with their lights flashing. No sirens, just lights. Officers were clustered on the street, weapons drawn.

I pulled up to the officers, rolled down my window, and asked if I could exit onto Constitution Avenue.

"No, sir", came the curt but respectful reply from the young man calmly waving me on. *"You'll need to exit off 15th Street."*

No explanation was offered, none was expected.

After years working amongst the professionals of the United States Secret Service Uniform Division, I have absolute faith in them. At that time, on that night, I knew I was safe, and the best thing for me to do was follow their directions.

As I made my way the half mile back around the top of the Ellipse to the 15th Street exit, I saw officer after officer on full alert, all with semi-automatic rifles at the ready.

So much for a quiet moment in a quiet place.

I drove onward through D.C. and went to my friend's party without knowing whether it was real or a drill, and until now in this book, I never said anything more about it. To me, it was just another high alert incident handled professionally by the Secret Service.

But it was not a drill. That night a disturbed young man from Idaho fired seven shots into the upper level of the White House residence, crashed his car a few blocks away, leaving his semi-automatic rifle behind in the wreckage, and fled unseen into the night.

Fortunately, no one was hurt. President Obama and the First Lady were in California at the time. But Sasha Obama and Mrs. Obama's mother, Marian Robinson, were inside the residence. Malia Obama, out with friends, was on her way home.

I wasn't hurt, none of the officers on the ground, or the rooftop observation post were injured. No staff were hurt. Miraculously no civilians were hurt that night or subsequently.

The White House exterior sustained some bullet damage, but the biggest casualty was the Obamas' trust in their protective perimeter.

While the gunman was eventually caught, and sentenced to 25 years in prison, the Secret Service Uniform Division was castigated for missing important clues during the incident that allowed the gunman to evade arrest for several days.

Rightfully, the Obamas and White House staffers were shaken by the incident. This was gun violence directed at them, in their house, the People's House.

They were targets. The White House was a target. Like in a video game. Or an overblown action movie.

I was almost a casualty. A couple of minutes sooner, and I would have driven right into the gunman's line of fire. His shooting position was within yards of my exit onto Constitution Avenue.

I never heard gunfire. Nor was I alerted about any as I passed the guard shack. That quiet, beautiful night had become sinister in a matter of minutes. I wouldn't learn the reason for it until days later.

A disturbed young man, drove thousands of miles across the country, and in a span of about 15 seconds, fired his legally purchased semi-automatic gun out of his car window with the intent of killing our president.

Up until the moment he pulled the trigger, he had broken none of our laws and was as entitled to every constitutionally protected right as you and I.

But he had a deranged idea, and in a regrettable instant he had acted on it. No telling how that idea formed within his troubled mind. But he'll spend years in jail because of his actions.

Thank God no one was hurt.

My beautiful wife grew up in England, a country that knows better than to idolize violent movies, television shows, and video games.

Though we disagree, she pointedly, on President Trump, which is her right as a naturalized American citizen, I trust her judgment on every aspect of civilized behavior. Reports of mass shootings in our country prompt the same reaction from her, she blames the media.

Neither pro-gun nor anti-gun, she is a peace-loving, anti-violence mom. Her objective eyes see the media's promotion of violent content to children as the root cause of America's gun culture.

With scant media promotion, and restrictive gun laws, England has no gun culture. Even counting England within the United Kingdom as a whole, the U.K.'s gun murder and gun suicide rates are minuscule compared to

America's. That's per capita, not overall.

Ironically though, reaching back in time, England's oppressive tactics in our colonial era are why we have our First and Second Amendments.

I understand responsible gun ownership and how that important right is protected by the Second Amendment. I understand responsible free speech and how that important right is protected by the First Amendment.

So does Joe Biden. Too bad he is bowing to his party's Hollywood donors and keeping his objections of their violent dehumanizing content to himself.

I doubt Joe Biden or his Democratic Party have the conviction to speak and act authentically on gun violence. They didn't in 2013, and they haven't changed since then.

In my opinion, if there is a bipartisan deal to address America's scourge of mass shootings, I believe Donald Trump will be the one to engineer it.

If my kids have to wait till their 18th birthday to play violent video games, and those laws are as strictly enforced as our gun laws or our tobacco laws, I can live with that. I know my wife can.

I think we all can.

And if you want to know if Joe Biden will take a win-or-lose stand on his Hollywood donors' contribution to gun violence, just ask him.

I would phrase it like this: *How do you feel about those violent content Hollywood guys, Joe? Really, how do you feel about them?*

Joe Will Do Iraq

CHAPTER SEVEN

J oe Biden loves warriors but hates war.

Well, actually he hates wars that weren't *his* idea.

To hear him tell it, which I did on several occasions, it was his relentless hectoring that pushed President Clinton to agree to our military intervention in the Bosnian war. This conflict ended with no American casualties and a peace agreement, and so it is a "successful" war Joe still brags about his role in promoting.

So more to the point, Joe hates wars that weren't his idea, like Afghanistan and Iraq (even though he voted *for both*).

But after voting and supporting those two wars (like a lot of us did), he started to really hate them.

But it's hard to hate something like war, and yet love the people doing that something. Americans (and our allies) found ourselves in a tough, drawn out and difficult series of regional wars from 2002 till — well, to be honest, we're still in them to this date.

Aren't we?

One thing I've learned over the course of my White House years about first-order conflicts and disasters, whether real or phony, is that those who practice the dark arts of politics manipulate the public's passions around them with gusto.

Joe Biden was clear (almost) that he loved the troops but hated the wars in Iraq and Afghanistan. He was clear (almost) about that as a senator. He was clear (almost) about that as Barack Obama's running mate in 2008.

But if you're a Democrat, the four most haunting words uttered over the last 20 years have to be Barack Obama's direction at the outset of his administration: *Joe will do Iraq.*

Because once Barack Obama turned the management of the Iraq war over to Joe Biden (in an Oval Office meeting that Joe loves boasting about), it became the foreign policy disaster that cost Hillary Clinton, Barack Obama and the Democrats dearly in 2016.

And the fallout that we're still suffering means they will continue to pay for it in 2020, as well.

Joe Biden loves American warriors. He loves our service members and those of our allies. He loves being out in the field amongst them. He loves the families who support them. And when he speaks of them, or to them, his words ring true.

But he was tragically careless in the drawdown of the Iraq war.

By saying this, I am not addressing that Joe gets a little jumbly with his recollections. Which he does. Regularly.

But regardless of the contradicting details and facts of his stories, he's consistent about his feelings.

In the six and a half years I worked for him, in speech after speech, fundraiser remarks after fundraiser remarks, interview after interview, he spoke in heartfelt terms of his experiences as a political leader in a country at war.

He feels it in his bones the loss of our troops. *Fallen Angels* is what he calls them, and he speaks movingly of accompanying a flag-draped casket on a long, somber flight back from Afghanistan.

He's not jumbly about that — because it happened, he was there, and he felt it.

I do not for one second deny that Joe Biden doesn't personally feel the loss of our service members. I do not for one second deny that Joe Biden didn't, and doesn't, personally feel what the families of our fallen service members feel.

And I say this not just because of how he says these things in interviews or onstage, but of how he acts when no one is around. In Joe's shirt pocket he carries a card which he instructs his staff to update every day with the exact — exact, not rounded off — number of American war fatalities to that date because, as he says, it matters.

Joe Biden knows that for the family members, friends, and comrades of our fallen service members, these facts mean a great deal, and that's why he holds fast to that daily ritual.

It's not score-keeping. Joe, like few others in a position of his political importance, reaches out with words of comfort and genuine concern for grieving family members.

I know this because, so often, I was there. Having heard just about every public statement he made as vice president, I am forever grateful for how he courageously shared his personal grief with Gold Star families at the TAPS, Tragedy Assistance Program for Survivors, ceremony on May 25, 2012.

His explanation of overcoming the loss of his wife, Neilia, and one-year-old daughter, Naomi, who were killed in a car accident on December 18, 1972, was a lifeline of encouragement to those devastated families.

"That's when you know you're going to make it", he told a hushed and anguished group who very much feared being consumed by their own grief. *"That's when you know you're going to make it."*

That gem of a speech is on YouTube.[16] You will be a better American if you watch it. The best part is what Joe says about Jill.

Wars require bravery, loyalty, and dedication from the men and women who fight them, and Joe Biden understands this.

He speaks with affectionate awe of seeing in person the dedication of troops in Afghanistan wiping their comrades' blood off the seats of their Humvees after a firefight, then saddling back up and going back out on patrol.

He speaks like he does because he's been there with them — watching, listening, joking, encouraging— so many times.

His wife, Jill, loves our service members, veterans, and their families. She and Michelle Obama co-founded *Joining Forces,*[17] a very successful White House initiative to support service members and their families.

Both she and Joe worked hard for our troops, our veterans, and their families in ways large and small.

Joe's son Beau left a prominent position as the attorney general of Delaware to volunteer with the Delaware Army National Guard. He served in Iraq with distinction, which made Joe and Jill and all their family justifiably proud and yet fraught with worry during his tour.

(Beau's brother, Hunter, tested positive for cocaine use while in the Navy Reserve in 2013 and was discharged in 2014. No deeper shame for a Biden.)

I traveled to Iraq three times with the White House — once with Dick Cheney in 2005 and twice with Joe Biden in 2011 and 2016. I saw and felt the enormous sacrifice our armed forces were making, but I also saw and felt the politics at the heart of that enormous sacrifice.

When you work in the White House as long as I did, and with the variety of people I did, you realize the extent to which everyone around you — Republican, Democrat, or Trumper — views everything in the world, including its wars, through the prism of politics.

And I say prism, not lens, because far from being clarified like the effect of a good lens, the view inside such a political environment is subject to prism-like distortions.

I certainly heard the reasons for the wars in Iraq and Afghanistan offered by President George W. Bush and his team.

Then I heard President Barack Obama and his team promise to end these wars.

Then I heard President Donald Trump and his team promise to resolve them, which in my opinion he has largely kept — his White House appears to be on a path to success in the Middle East.

But we'll see. President Trump's decision to greenlight the drone strike[18] on Iranian General Qasem Soleimani, which I fully support, could have unforeseen ramifications in the future for good or ill.

But now on the campaign trail for the 2020 election we hear former Vice President Joe Biden asking us to believe only he can end the "forever wars".

Really, Joe? Didn't you already "do" Iraq once?

My knowledge of Joe's "doing" of Iraq starts with me accompanying him on a trip in December 2011 with the goal of bringing about a cessation of hostilities there, which was timed specifically to lead into Barack Obama's 2012 re-election effort.

Our trip began with a secretive flight to Iraq on an unmarked C-17 that was, with the vice president aboard, designated Air Force Two.

Joe was scheduled to meet with Iraqi leaders in the Green Zone, make a ringing speech to an assembly of Iraqi and American troops at Al Faw Palace, and then fly to Erbil for a face-to-face meeting with Masoud Barzani, the leader of the Kurds in Iraq.

At the time, for Joe Biden, the self-proclaimed White House Optimist, this was a triumphant trip.

Why wouldn't it be? He was *the* newsmaker of the best news story in years. His son Beau was home from Iraq, reunited with his family. A terrible war looked less terrible. Best of all, Joe was about to gift the families of 150,000 service members a no-more-combat reunion with their loved ones.

So much winning.

After an overnight — relatively quiet, no rocket attacks — stay at the heavily fortified U.S. embassy in Baghdad, Joe had an emotional interview with Ann Curry, then of NBC's *Today Show* at the ambassador's residence.

Curry, who had lost her brother due to an in-service vehicle accident while he was serving in the Air Force years prior to the Iraq war, had a deep empathy for the Gold Star families of the Iraq and Afghanistan era. Ann and Joe had an emotional connection during the interview over the matter of the coming conclusion of years of conflict in Iraq.

Ever the astute journalist, Curry was dutifully tough on Biden, asking if Iraq was ready for the U.S. to leave and whether or not the Iraq war was a victory.

Joe's reply encapsulated Team Obama's attitude: Carelessness borne of arrogance.

"What we're claiming here", said Joe, "is that we've done the job our administration set out to do, to end a war we did not start, to end it in a responsible way to bring Americans home, to end the bleeding — both financially and physically — that this war has caused, and to leave in place the prospect of a trained military, under democratic institutions."[19]

Plausible words at the time, but that was eight atrocity-filled years, hundreds of thousands of civilian casualties, and a litany of excuses ago.

Carelessness borne of arrogance.

Recall that jubilant applause line — *"we ended two wars"* — from all those 2012 campaign speeches? I do. Joe Biden delivered it into my earphones so many times I occasionally hear it in my sleep.

"Ended" is what he said.

Well, that applause line worked as planned. The election went to Obama. The anti-war voters were jubilant.

But it was all a concocted mirage. In actuality, Afghanistan was never over. Neither was Iraq.

Former Secretaries of Defense Bob Gates and James Mattis have both been extremely critical of Joe Biden's carelessness with the cessation of hostilities. And while they are circumspect, I'm not: Joe Biden ignored repeated warnings about overdoing the U.S. troop pullout and thousands of Iraqis and Syrians paid for his arrogance with their lives.

The proof of that is the ugly eruption of ISIS, a group of radical Islamic terrorists neither President Obama nor Vice President Biden understood.

Obama called them *"a JV team"*.[20] But then this "JV team" was in Mosul, Ramadi, Fallujah, Basra, Tikrit, and it was disgusting that so many places so many Americans had sacrificed so much for were now back in the hands of a deadly enemy.

Carelessness borne of arrogance.

As I write this, the world is still digesting the news of the death of high ranking Iranian terrorist Qassem Soleimani. Add to that the successful raid to eliminate the ISIS caliph al-Baghdadi last fall, and we all owe President Trump, his operational teams, and our brave commandos a heartfelt thanks for making our world more safe.

Under President Trump's orders, they have eliminated mass murderers with stunning efficiency. Amazing that so many begrudge them a simple thank you for that accomplishment.

Compare that to how Joe Biden and Barack Obama mismanaged the rise of ISIS and the war on terror in Iraq (though eliminating Osama bin Laden in Pakistan was certainly one of their best days).

Even to a lenient press, Team Obama struggled to explain how it was they had ended anything while there was rising bloodshed in Iraq, Afghanistan, Syria, Yemen, and Libya. Essentially, from 2012 on, starting with the murky tragedy of the Benghazi incident, drone attacks and bombings under President Obama and Vice President Joe Biden's leadership increased.

And while the reporting on Benghazi has been extensive, as it should be, the arguments over Team Obama's handling of it remain as virulent as ever. There are so many unanswered questions.

Likewise, the reporting on Team Obama's mishandling of the ISIS breakout in Iraq in summer 2014 has also left far too many questions unanswered, with the main one being: *Why did you leave so quickly when the Iraqi army was so unprepared?*

I've never heard any national security pronouncement as stupid as Team Obama's national security expert Tony Blinken's assertion, 'We *had to leave Iraq, so they would trust us to come back.*'

Really, Tony? That was your plan. Entrust all our American military's surplus weapons and vehicles to the Iraqi army so they could hand them over to ISIS and then beg us to come back and save them from those same weapons?

To those of us who heard this it was insultingly dumb. Thank the advocacy media for underreporting that, too.

My third visit to Iraq (my second one with Joe) was in spring 2016, and this was also timed with another election. It was meant to shore up the

Obama administration's plummeting foreign policy credibility ahead of the November 2016 contest between Obama's former Secretary of State Hillary Clinton and Republican candidate Donald Trump.

This was the "ISIS, we're coming" for you trip. If the "yes, we ended it" claims after the 2011 trip had been honest, the 2016 trip would not have been necessary.

The reality is that in 2016, Vice President Biden's brief visit with the Kurds in Erbil required the highest security environment I have ever seen in 15 years of White House travel.

In 2011, we had breezed into Erbil, traveling from the airport to Barzani's heavily guarded compound in a standard motorcade. There were no military vehicles in sight, only police cars. We were riding through Iraq with the Vice President of the United States in exactly the same manner as if we were traveling through Ohio on our way to Columbus.

But in 2016, we traveled that same short distance to Barzani's compound by helicopter, with a Special Ops escorts on the helos and in the two-minute motorcade — hard-eyed men, heavy weapons, security eight layers deep. At one point, the Special Forces guys held us back in the helo, not allowing us to board Air Force Two for departure, while they checked out the deep grass at the edge of the runway.

I've been in and out of combat zones for years. This time I felt as if, long after being told that the war "ended," the enemy was right there in our laps.

It was disgusting to follow Joe Biden into Iraq for another White House publicity tour promoting another U.S.-led military campaign, especially when our troops were fighting to regain territory their comrades had already sacrificed for.

Now Barack Obama's former vice president is out there talking about his credentials to be elected president so he can end the Forever Wars.

Really, Joe? Really?

Let me state the obvious, President Trump's management of the war on terror that he inherited has been far superior than what his predecessors Bush or Obama put in place.

To me, President Donald Trump's stark appraisal of President Bush's decision to enter into the wars in Afghanistan and Iraq as being the *"worst single mistake in our country's history"*[21] is the most accurate expression yet of our national hatred of war.

It has taken me a lot of soul searching to say that. I worked in George W. Bush's White House. I was there in the midst of his team's efforts justifying and promoting those wars. I volunteered at Walter Reed Army Medical Center and watched the school buses bringing in the wounded. As part of my job I traveled to military installations all around the world. I have only admiration and respect for our military.

Because of that environment it was easy for me to not see things that are apparent to me now. I needed a long time before I would agree that President Bush's decision was a terrible mistake. I believed war was the right course then, but I don't now.

Trump is right, but the mistake isn't all encompassing. Americans did gain something from the Iraq and Afghanistan wars: We learned even more that we hate our wars, but we love our warriors.

Out of all the anguish and sacrifice, those wars helped us see that.

The individual heroism our military operations in the Middle East granted to hundreds of thousands of Americans — male and female — who served as our protectors is real, honorable and immeasurable.

From the time I started with the Bush administration, war was the dominant issue of my entire 15-year span in the White House. On this topic I would only say this: Every American needs to make their own peace with the whys of what war has become in our time.

We can't afford to be naive about America's role in world peace. The president of the United States is the leader of the free world because our military is global like no one else's. They are the toughest, most competent arbiters of international fairness in hostile situations the world has ever seen. Not perfect, but far better than anything else out there.

We all have our truths, beliefs, and opinions about our wars and our warriors. I will share with you another man's war story that helped me accept my truths.

I met Bill when I was volunteering at Walter Reed Army Medical Center (WRAMC) in the Bush years.

Some kayaking friends and I had put together a volunteer program of kayak therapy at Walter Reed, and I got to know Bill as I drove him back and forth from the hospital to the Potomac River for kayaking excursions.

Bill was a Vietnam war veteran, infantryman, older than me by a few years, with twinkling blue eyes, a ready smile, and legs that ended just above his knees.

Bill was a warrior in a wheelchair. He had lived that truth for most of his life.

But that was about to change. He was down at WRAMC from Pennsylvania because he had heard that with technology advances, the new prosthetics were worth having, as opposed to what he had been offered in the past as a warrior for a country that did not then love its warriors.

Vietnam-era vets recall how they were mistreated. Bill remembered. He had given a lot to the Army, and to his country, and even though he had to wait three decades, he was going to get the quality prosthetics he deserved.

So during his outfitting period for his new legs, Bill joined in with our kayak therapy program, Team River Runner.[22]

We thought we were "helping" him. Not at all. *He was helping us.*

Bill was broad-chested and independent. He moved out of his chair and into our transport van with the agility of a gymnast, cheerfully declining assistance — not because he didn't want it, but because he didn't need it.

All we had to do to assist him was fold up his chair and put it in the back of the van, and then pull it out at the destination so he could self-sufficiently maneuver himself into it.

But when he did need transport assistance, like when we half-wheeled, half-carried him over rocky, uneven trails to get to the river bank, he was gentle in his reminders that the load we were carrying was a human being who did not want to be dropped.

There's a vulnerability to someone who relies on a wheelchair. Bill taught me that.

Between his can-do attitude and congenial ways, Bill became the go-to elder for the younger vets in the program. There are life lessons of living with war injuries, and Bill passed those on freely and fully.

He loved the kayaking. We had a boat outfitted especially for him, so once he was on the water, settled into his boat, and fitted on his spraydeck, he was every inch the kayaker any of us were. His kayak became like his wheelchair, only this time no one saw his injuries.

I think that was a comfort for him.

We did a lot of boating. He loved it — the outdoorsy thrill. We'd all set off together for the adventure of the next rapid. Old vets, young vets, volunteers — paddling, laughing, talking. Simple fun.

In my 15 years at the White House, my experience guiding Bill and his comrades to health and healing with Team River Runner is the memory

I cherish most. There is no higher honor than serving those who served.

Gradually as Bill got to know us, he shared more and more about his life since his injury. Not because we asked, but because he was surrounded by folks who appreciated what he had been through.

He hadn't been supported like that when he returned from his war.

So were there limitations? I wouldn't use that word with Bill. I don't think he knew what it meant.

Bill liked to hunt, and told me of the time he went to Colorado to hunt elk from horseback. The mobility worked fine, but apparently riding a big furry animal through a Colorado forest in elk season had its risks.

Count on Bill to come up with a solution. *"That was fun"*, he chuckled in the telling. *"But we had to cover that horse in a swath of blaze orange from nose to tail"*.

The story of Bill's I liked best — and he told it just once — spoke volumes about the ornery pride and can-do attitude that makes our American warriors the best in the world, why they're unbeatable, why they get the job done, and why when the military is as dumb as it sometimes is, they figure out a way to make it less dumb.

It's also why we love them.

"When I got back from 'Nam, I was recovering in a VA hospital in San Francisco", Bill said, holding me with a direct gaze that made it clear he didn't want my pity. *"And they weren't treating us well"*, he added.

Then he paused, took a breath and continued.

"So we improvised. One night me and another guy got the keys to one of the vans in the motor pool", Bill said, cracking a grin. *"Neither of us had legs so we couldn't reach the pedals to drive. But that night, we were getting out of that hospital.*

"What we did was, one of us sat in the driver's seat while the other guy was down on the floor pushing the pedals with his hands".

At this point Bill was chuckling. *"So the driver's seat guy is calling out the instructions — gas, brake, gas, brake — and steering us out for a night on the town while the floor guy is working the pedals."*

Bill was smiling broadly at the memory of their one-night triumph. He didn't tell me much more about it. I didn't ask. I didn't have to. I only had to know that some 40 years later, he was as proud as ever of his great escape into the San Francisco night. He should be. That's a good war story.

A few years after telling me that story, Bill moved to Tucson, Arizona, where he spent his last days.

Rest In Peace, Bill. You were a hero for everyone who knew you and all the rest of your countrymen who didn't.

The political finger pointing over these forever wars and who voted, and who didn't, and who lied, and who didn't, and who actually ended them, and who didn't, is tearing our country apart.

As bad as these forever wars have been for our great country, and for those countries where they've been waged, I think as Americans, we can all finally agree on one thing, and Bill's war story exemplifies it.

Mike McCormick, solo stenographer supporting Vice President Dick Cheney, Al-Asa Air Base, Iraq, December 18, 2005. (White House/David Bohrer)

After the travesty of the mistreatment of our returning Vietnam vets, we, citizens of the United States, are now united in supporting our service members and their families.

We, all of us, love our warriors. We have put the self-hatred of Vietnam war era to rest. *We still hate war, but we love our warriors.*

And as that country that loves its warriors, we need a commander-in-chief who can lead our indispensable nation by being clear, honest, and direct with us about why we need to wage a war, all the while knowing what it will do to the warriors we love. We need a commander-in-chief who is decisive and lethal — no matter how much criticism that generates.

Joe Biden loves the troops, but he was indecisive and careless in their drawdown. Chaos, suffering and death are his legacy in Iraq.

He will never be our commander-in-chief.

Everything But The Flying Monkeys

CHAPTER EIGHT

Politicians crave an audience.

And when politicians crave an audience as badly as Joe Biden has for as long as he has, sometimes it gets *weird*. After working for over 15 years with presidents and vice presidents, I have seen that there are things they say and ways they act in public that demonstrate that regardless of political affiliation, they understand what's expected of them when appearing before their fellow citizens. I would have thought Joe would understand that. *But he doesn't.*

April 15, 2013, Vice President Joe Biden was at his West Wing desk on a conference call with Boston police officials. They were speaking in a jocular tone as befitted a pleasant afternoon conversation between a group of men who loved the prestige of being high-ranking civil servants. Joe was drumming up support for his gun violence task force, and the police officials were honored by his call.

It's important to note here that whenever he was at his desk in the White House, directly across from him was a television tuned to a cable news network (but *definitely not* Fox).

A few minutes into the meeting, Vice President Joe Biden spoke what in my 15 years of listening to White House officials was the most bizarre thing I ever heard.

Joe was speaking to this group of officials primarily about the threat of mass casualty events, like mass shootings, when in what sounded like a throw-off line, he said something to the effect of, *yeah, I think we're fine unless there's a bombing or something.*

Recall the date: April 15, 2013.

Recall the audience: Boston police officials.

Recall the phrase: *"Unless there's a bombing or something".*

At that moment Joe Biden spoke those very words, he had begun to see on his television that there were news reports of explosions happening at the Boston Marathon finish line.

I was given a recording of the meeting shortly afterward by Biden's staffers, and while listening to it I heard in the background the concerned, heightened voices of other people reacting to the television report. Then the next phrase out of the Vice President's mouth is something like: *"Hey, something just came across the television screen! I've got to jump."*

Instant hang up, end of call, end of recording.

But, talk about an unsettling, self-fulfilling prophecy!

It was eerie that he would say the phrase *"unless there's a bombing or something"*, at the exact same moment that the ghastly bombing attack in Boston was happening.

Because the audio didn't originate from the good folks at WHCA, my transcript is the only record of that call. Nor were there any press listening in, so this incident was never publicly disclosed. But I guarantee it exists. Doubters can verify my version of this episode through a FOIA request of the transcript I emailed back to Joe's staffers.

As neither Joe nor anyone else has ever spoken publicly about this, my account is all there is.

So far.

But that peculiar coincidence is in its own category, because there's an area of Joe Biden's public speaking that is actually disturbing in a whole different way. I'm talking about the things he says that are downright *creepy*.

When it came to him saying cringe-worthy stuff, especially in regards to women and gays, yes, definitely, these things happened — over and over and over. Not because what he said was demeaning or derogatory, but rather how he said it was, well, *creepy*.

One topic that was guaranteed to get Joe Biden ranting and raving was his authorship of the Violence Against Women Act (VAWA)[23] when he was a senator. He spoke of that often and at length.

Joe was proud of his decades of work on behalf of women and children who needed a stronger safety net to help them escape domestic violence. He should be. *His work saved lives.*

This work got him a standing ovation at the 2016 Academy Awards ceremony when he introduced the famous singer Lady Gaga and asked viewers to take the pledge to eliminate campus sexual assault on the *It's On Us* website. Well deserved.

Joe was proud of his work to fund full testing of rape kits long neglected in police station evidence rooms due to overworked staff and insufficient budgets. Immediately, cases were solved with DNA testing, science providing a tool for justice that is unemotional, a nonracial arbiter without bias. Criminals were jailed with certainty. Victims were unburdened with certainty. Lives were saved. Justice was well served.

His work in this area also paid off with Hollywood attention. In 2016 he made a cameo appearance on the TV crime drama *Law and Order: SVU* opposite the star of the show, Mariska Hargitay.[24] Mariska is a big supporter of the effort to eliminate the back log of untested rape kits,[25] and she and Vice President Biden became great friends.

I dreaded the VAWA events, and it wasn't just me. I heard nearly every single speech Joe gave, but in this area and on this topic, Joe was at his best *and worst*. Best because of his mastery of an emotional issue, worst for how he conveyed it. The young women in my office who adored Barack Obama could not stand hearing these speeches by Joe.

As the Vice President spoke about violence against women his demeanor changed dramatically, becoming overbearing and enraged. Theatrically it seemed to me. Time and time again, I was offended by the emotional manipulation of his speech, thundering at the top of his voice, *"No means no!"*

He knew he was making his audience uncomfortable. He could see it in their faces. Then he'd apologize for his intensity, excusing himself for being passionate. But as someone who heard him address this topic over and over, it was disturbing, and I certainly wasn't the only person who felt this way.

Just about every time he spoke on it, he would soon be yelling — screaming really — at imaginary people who didn't understand that no means no means no; that rape wasn't always with a stranger; that young men were cowards for not deterring a sexual assault; that a woman should never be blamed for "what she was wearing"; that the worst sin was a man raising his hand to a woman or child — that this was an abuse of power.

His assertions were vital and unchallengeable, but screaming them at his audience in this manner was primal, unnerving, and ultimately *creepy*.

Presidents don't scream — at least not in public. Not like that. After a career in public service that had begun over four decades ago,[26] Joe's behavior was mystifying for its lack of self-restraint, particularly for a public figure in such a high position of power who had an ambition to rise even higher.

Witnessing him shouting his denunciations against rape was not the worst of it, for the creepiest part of his VAWA messages were his imitations of frightened women calling into domestic abuse hotlines. Making a strangely voiced characterization, he would portray threatened women in a fashion so upsetting my female colleagues refused to work with the recordings we made.

But that wasn't Joe's only creepy voice imitation.

For some reason, in the later stages of the administration, when he'd speak to LGBTQ groups, proclaiming the advancement of our society toward being more open-minded and inclusive, his story-telling would include imitating a man speaking *in a falsetto voice*. If you heard him do this repeatedly, as I did, it would bother you as much as it bothered me, raising questions that went beyond whether Joe's intentions were good but his execution was awkward, into what he thought people were really like.

During his presentations before groups, time and again, in the process of describing how Team Obama had helped America grow more accepting of LGTBQ rights, he would employ this theatrical device of pretending to be other people. In this case, Joe would portray a party of business people at lunch who would disapprove of one of their own group insulting a male waiter who, because he spoke with a lisp, was presented in Joe's story as obviously gay.

Then he'd imitate the diner insultingly imitating the waiter in a falsetto voice that was, again, quite *creepy* and gave off that same feeling one gets when viewing some long lost photograph of a famous liberal politician in blackface.

Over time, in the course of witnessing Joe Biden stump speeches, I learned there was always an added ingredient that came with these portrayals of the pretend-people he invented — anger — lots of it. He preferred to call this "passion", but that passion seemed to always work in one direction against one kind of person. His righteous indignation about unequal treatment of women, minorities, and the middle class was perpetrated by one kind of villain, and in Joe's telling they always seemed to be *Republicans.*

I think Joe believed he was speaking appropriately, but sometimes he would work himself into a such a rant his reasonable audience members could only laugh nervously and shake their heads.

Joe's raving about Republicans were legendary in Democratic Party circles. His favorite theme was that Republicans were incapable of understanding everyday Americans. *"These guys don't get it",* he'd say, mostly to his Middle Class Joe audiences in Pennsylvania, Ohio, and Wisconsin — the very folks Barack Obama avoided talking to in the later stages of his presidency.

He had a whole shtick about being "middle class in America", which he rolled out with the practiced precision of a car salesman describing an economy model's most dependable features.

He'd proclaim it at campaign rallies and fundraisers, insisting Republicans have no insight into the struggles of the middle class.[27]

And there were those in the audiences who ate this up, until Donald Trump arrived on the scene. In 2016, though Trump was the former donor to so many of Joe's Democratic friends, he became Joe's new object of derision. Ironically, at the same time Joe began to attack him, those middle class audiences begun to switch their attention to what Donald Trump was saying.

And they still are.

I recall one rant from Joe that dripped with class envy. His recollection of an interaction with one of the uber-wealthy DuPont kids he knew from his high school days in Wilmington, Delaware, which Joe used as a springboard for vilifying the wealthy.

He'd talk about how he had known the DuPont family throughout his career, and he appreciated their status in Delaware. Joe would then launch into a recollection of a conversation he'd had in high school with one of the DuPont boys who was his age and had a nice car.

In Joe's telling he would mention that he had a car, a Packard, I think it was. In the story, he explained to this DuPont boy that he had to change the oil in his Packard. *"Why don't you have your man do it?"* the DuPont boy innocently asked.

Simple question. But Joe Biden used this to kick off into a tirade about wealth and privilege, and that this somehow showed how the aloof

Republicans ignore the middle class.

This attack on the DuPonts reflected a general change by Team Obama which now focused more on targeting "millionaires and billionaires". I do not know why they so drastically altered their message, but Joe seemed to especially relish this kind of attack.

However, Joe being Joe, every once in a while he forget himself and would start ranting against the very wealthy while talking *to* the very wealthy. His message would put him siding with the Occupy Wall Street kids against the Wall Street donors he wanted to support his campaign.

Not smart, Joe. First you bash the rich folks *then* you ask them for dough?

As Barack Obama would say, *come on, man.*

But these aren't simply events where Joe made momentary gaffes. His diatribes were repeated so often they became predictable.

On another date I was listening in by audio linkup to a fundraiser for Chuck Schumer and Chuck was running late, so Joe jumped up on stage to fill time by sharing his thoughts with the high-dollar Manhattanites who were Schumer's donors. Thirty minutes later his spontaneous talk has built up into an angry attack on them, the intensity rising in his voice like he's about to start throwing punches, telling them about how they have to start *"paying their share"*.

Ridiculous.

Listening to the proceedings on a live WHCA audio feed in my EEOB[28] office, I could hear the audience stiffening in annoyance. I've had enough experience with fundraisers over the years to know that *this is not the way to talk to donors.*

Finally, Schumer arrived in a breathless rush. Annoyed at the mistreatment of his donors, he went straight to the microphone and wrestled it away from Joe, ending the rant.

But these episodes with Joe produced one single question that was self-answering: how is that presidential?

But this weird, self-defeating behavior isn't just an expression of a peculiar communication style, because linked to this is that Joe Biden has some pretty *weird* ideas, too.

Donors and Drug Dealers

CHAPTER NINE

P revious chapters have examined Joe's foreign policy bona fides, which upon closer inspection are actually rather rickety outside of benefiting Hollywood. But nothing sums up Joe Biden's wrongheaded misjudgment of foreign policy than his oft-repeated belief that the key to unlocking peace in the Middle East was to solve the decades-old crisis in Cyprus.

Cyprus? That island in the Mediterranean?[29] Really, Joe? *Cyprus?*

Yes, you read that right, and you are forgiven if you can't follow the connection. Not many would.

The only possible way to understand this is to know the important fact that, as Joe has said many times, his earliest and most loyal donors are Greek Americans. I personally heard him say so, numerous times, that this group has been behind him from the start, and he has always treasured their support.

What Joe *has not said*, though, is what those donors want. The 1974 Turkish invasion of Cyprus resulted in the island being divided into a Greek-Cypriot Zone and a Turkish-Cypriot Zone. In international law, though, the island itself is an independent state separate from Turkey and Greece, divided with a heavily-fortified border, with a majority of

Greek-speaking people on one side and a minority of Turkish-speaking people on the other.

The outcome in 1974 was a bitter blow to the government of Greece which was seeking a reunion of Cyprus with the Greek "mother state", something which Turkey, of course, absolutely didn't, and still doesn't, want to have happen. The result of the fighting in 1974 was that Turkey moved military units to the island, the Greek government under Dimitrios Ioannidis collapsed, and only massive pressure from the United States and Europe kept the fighting from enlarging from Cyprus into a war across the entire eastern Mediterranean.

The conflicts between Turkey and Greece go back many centuries, to the fall of Constantinople[30] in 1453, and it is not a simple matter between the two countries in any area of contact, let alone Cyprus. Over 40 years since the 1974 invasion of the island, with many negotiations and peace-talks, Cyprus is still divided. Neither side has budged enough to end the stalemate.

But Joe's Greek American donors wanted Joe to fix it *their way,* so through the power of the Office of the Vice President he worked it, and he worked it, and he *worked it some more.*

But for whom? We Americans? Or for the Greeks? Or the Turks? Or his donors?

More questions come up when you realize that Burisma Holdings[31] may figure into Joe's interest in Cyprus.

That's right — Burisma Holdings figures directly into this.

While it may not be widely known, it is no secret that Joe Biden made a concerted effort to conduct personal outreach to the leaders of Cyprus,

Greece, and Turkey over the course of his vice presidency. He made phone calls, had meetings in Washington and elsewhere, and coordinated diplomatic outreach.

Joe also traveled to Turkey and Greece many times. I accompanied him on several of those trips.

Then in May 2014, Joe Biden made a very unusual four-day trip. First, he went to Romania, then Cyprus. What made this trip notable was that it was the first visit to the island of Cyprus by a senior American official since Vice President Lyndon Johnson stopped there in 1962. But despite this history-making visit, no American press were brought along, and my usual job of recording for Joe wasn't needed, so I didn't go either. Joe's mission was to talk about reunification on Cyprus, Russia's invasion of Ukraine, and European energy security.[32]

Wait, *Ukraine?*

Sure. Why not? Especially since Ukraine's largest natural gas company, Burisma Holdings, while headquartered in Kyiv, *was registered in Cyprus.*

Wait, May 2014?

Sure. Why not? Especially since sketchy Ukrainian oligarch Mykola Zlochevsky, who ran sketchy Burisma Holdings — you know, the company that had just weeks before benefited from an aid package Joe delivered on his trip to Kyiv — was then living in Cyprus, *that probably had nothing to do with Joe's visit.*

Probably not. Nah!

And as far as the possibility that Zlochevsky and Vice President Biden met or spoke to each other, or had their staffers speak to each other while the two were literally just miles apart on a nondescript island, far from prying eyes. Again, *probably not.*

This despite that they were in the same place at the same time — a place renowned for money laundering activities — and both deeply connected to boosting natural gas development in Ukraine.

So did Joe set up a money laundering account in Cyprus? That would be another question he should answer.

Probably not. Nope!

But, *come on, man!*

Joe's arrival in Cyprus was just a week after Burisma Holdings' press release that publicly announced Joe's son Hunter was now a new board member. And now right nearby was Mykola Zlochevsky, the co-founder of that company which was directly being benefitted from the White House aid package that Joe Biden had led.

But, even with a list of coincidences like this promoting the obvious questions about possible collusion, or secret meetings, the facts have yet to be properly investigated. And, the hard reality is that on the Cyprus trip Joe's interest to work for peace between the Turk and Greek Cypriots went for naught.

Despite a lot of time and taxpayer money spent, there has been no discernible advance in the reunification of Cyprus due to Joe Biden's exhaustive efforts.

None. Zero. *Nada.*

Just when in 2016 it seemed like he was close to an actual resolution with

Greek-Cypriot President Nicos Anastasiades and Turkish-Cypriot leader Mustafa Akinci,[33] suddenly — poof, everything fizzled and a peace deal fell through. In 2020, as I write this, Cyprus is no closer to reunification than it was 1974.

I've never heard of the reasons Joe failed so miserably in Cyprus. No one has. But I suspect what happened is Turkish President Recep Tayyip Erdogan lost respect for Joe's ability to get things done. But we'll get to that later.

Unfortunately, the Obama years are littered with the wreckage of Joe Biden's botched "deals" that didn't come to pass or work out the way intended. Cyprus wasn't the only deal Joe pursued with passion and good intentions only to have it vaporize into obscurity, *or worse.*

Which brings us to his pet project, the *Alliance for Prosperity.* Joe's attention wasn't just on China, Ukraine, and Cyprus, but also the Northern Triangle countries of Guatemala, El Salvador, and Honduras.

Desperate to address the 2014 refugee crisis then happening along the United States' southern border, particularly the tragic and sudden influx of unaccompanied minors, the White House needed to act. At Joe's behest the Obama administration devised an optimistic, high-dollar aid program that, in the end, only made the situation worse.

Much worse.

To understand the abject futility of *Alliance for Prosperity,* you need only to start with the present and work back in time.

October, 2019 — with all the breathless reporting on the Democrats' impeachment inquiry and the death of al-Baghdadi, you would be excused if you missed the news stories on the drug trafficking conviction in a New York courtroom of Juan Antonio (Tony) Hernandez, who also happens to be the brother of the president of Honduras Juan Orlando Hernandez.

But what does this have to do with *Joe Biden?*

Sadly, for American taxpayers, a great deal indeed, because Joe Biden's *Alliance for Prosperity,* which to this day Joe continues to tout as a success that he played such an important part of, was responsible for throwing hundreds of millions of dollars at the cartel-infested Honduran government for years.

Here's a look at the Hondurans' narcotrafficking as described in a Department of Justice, U.S. Attorneys Office, Southern District of New York press release dated October 18, 2019:

> *"Manhattan U.S. Attorney Geoffrey S. Berman said:* 'Former Honduran congressman Tony Hernandez was involved in all stages of the trafficking through Honduras of multi-ton loads of cocaine that were destined for the U.S... Hernandez stands convicted of his crimes and faces the possibility of a lengthy prison sentence ... Hernandez is a former member of the National Congress of Honduras, the brother of the current President of Honduras, and a large-scale drug trafficker who worked with other drug traffickers in, among other places, Colombia, Honduras, and Mexico, to import cocaine into the United States.
>
> 'From at least in or about 2004, up to and including in or about 2018, Hernandez helped process, receive, transport, and distribute multi-ton loads of cocaine that arrived in Honduras via planes, helicopters, and go-fast vessels. Hernandez controlled cocaine laboratories in Honduras and Colombia,*

...in connection with these activities, Hernandez participated in the importation of almost 200,000 kilograms of cocaine into the United States.

'*Hernandez made millions of dollars through his cocaine trafficking, and he funneled millions of dollars of drug proceeds to National Party campaigns to impact Honduran presidential elections in 2009, 2013, and 2017. Between 2010 and at least 2013, one of Hernandez's principal co-conspirators was former Sinaloa Cartel leader Joaquin Archivaldo Guzman Loera, aka 'Chapo.' During that period, Hernandez helped Guzman Loera with numerous large cocaine shipments and delivered a $1 million bribe from Guzman Loera to Hernandez's brother in connection with the 2013 national elections in Honduras.*'" [34]

Tony Hernandez, who is appealing his conviction, is facing life in prison. His brother, Honduran President Juan Orlando Hernandez, named in the trial as an unindicted co-conspirator, denies any wrongdoing and is still the president of the country.

Got that? Narcotrafficking on a massive scale and at the highest levels of the Honduran government all while under Joe Biden's leadership his pet project was firehosing U.S. taxpayer cash into the country.

This financial program was meant to address the refugee crisis that caught Team Obama unaware in 2014. By funding this program in the Northern Triangle, the goal was to strengthen democracy, create stability, and add security for the inhabitants, and hopefully stem their desperate mass migration toward United States borders. This initiative included the effort to fight drug abuse and drug-trafficking, but in Honduras the American taxpayer funding was provided to President Juan Orlando Hernandez and his brother Juan Antonio Hernandez, *literally going to the narcotraffickers themselves.*

Oh, by the way, who sold Joe on this idea for an aid program for the Northern Triangle in the first place? It was cannily pitched as a small scale effort to imitate the bipartisan supported Plan Colombia[35] that operated from 2000-2015, and was originally signed into law by President Bill Clinton, and then backed by each succeeding president that followed.

This new plan to send $1.5 billion in funding into the Northern Triangle was proposed to Joe by none other than President Juan Orlando Hernandez!

Joe Biden continues to campaign to be our president on the lie that Alliance for Prosperity was a success, still bringing it up as late as November 2019. And while one of his favorite sayings is *"all politics is personal"*, I guarantee he's no longer bragging about his personal relationship with Juan Orlando Hernandez, the ongoing president of Honduras.

But in the waning days of the Obama administration, Joe was still loud and proud about his work with Honduras' unindicted co-conspirator president. On January 4, 2017, this was provided by the Office of the Vice President:

> *"The Vice President spoke with President Juan Orlando Hernandez of Honduras by telephone today to review progress on the implementation of the Alliance for Prosperity Plan for the Northern Triangle of Central America. The Vice President praised Honduras' progress in improving security and tax administration and urged continued commitment to combating corruption and upholding the rule of law. President Hernandez expressed his gratitude for the Vice President's sustained engagement with Central America and pledged his continuing efforts to advance prosperity, security, and governance in Honduras and the region."[36]*

Nice, flowery words, Joe. But really, were you fighting for the "soul of

America" then, as your 2020 campaign slogan would have Americans believe? Or were you selling it?

In fact, eight months after Joe offered that ringing endorsement, in another high-profile New York court case, *the son* of the former president of Honduras was sentenced to 23 years in prison after pleading guilty to drug trafficking.

Fabio Porfirio Lobo, whose father, Porfirio "Pepe" Lobo Sosa, was the previous president of Honduras — so daddy was the top guy right before unindicted co-conspirator Hernandez took over — was sentenced in September 2017 after having pled guilty to those charges in May 2016. So the activities of the dirty Hernandez brothers cannot be viewed as just appearing out of nowhere, but from an established pattern already known about the Honduran government well into Honduras' previous administration.

Hold up. That guy Fabio Porfirio Lobo pled guilty in May 2016? Isn't that at the same time when Joe and Barack were in office and giving our money to Honduras to fight crime?

Ay caramba!

Wasn't anyone on Joe Biden's staff capable of warning him against sending so much American cash to Central American governments, some of whose leaders were then under investigation by the DEA for drug dealing?

Apparently *not.*

By my math, Joe Biden + taxpayer dollars + assistance to Honduran narcotraffickers = criminal carelessness.

Not just careless, but bordering on ridiculously excessive, given the total population of those three countries is approximately only 31 million. Putting it another way, U.S. taxpayers ponied up about $48 per person (including children and infants) to the corrupt and ineffective governments of those three countries. For what?

From 2014 to 2016, Joe Biden's *Alliance for Prosperity* sent over $1.5 billion of U.S. aid to Honduras, El Salvador, and Guatemala. That's 1.5 billion *with a B* U.S. dollars flooding for three years into three tiny Central American countries infamous for *their three C's* — corruption, crime, and cartels.

Not a joke.

And the amount would have been higher except Congress cut Obama's funding request for the *Alliance for Prosperity* in 2016 down to $750 million from $1 billion.

So *only* $750 million in 2016. Wow.

But that 2016 number needs to be contrasted with what America had been doing before. The 2016 budget *doubled* U.S. assistance to Central America of $317 million from fiscal year 2014 and represented a big jump over the $560 million allocation from fiscal year 2015.

But for what purpose? To whom? That was a staggering $1.5 billion in three years. Does Joe to this day even understand the kind of government officials he was handing it over to? He can't have been oblivious to the narcotrafficking in the Honduras government, could he?

For a politician who brags about his foreign policy expertise as much as Joe, this is a train wreck that he engineered.

Utterly careless. The refugees are still coming. If the assistance money was simply a cash payment to influence the governments of the Northern Triangle countries to restrain their own people from fleeing to the USA, it did not work. Now, more than ever, the citizens of those three countries continue to exit with a goal of reaching the United States.

So what has the $1.5 billion that Team Obama handed over to prevent refugee migration from Northern Triangle countries accomplished?

American voters should be asking Joe that. I'm sure if they knew about it, they would.

And how about **The Washington Post** or **The New York Times?** Isn't their stated mission to be watchguards over activities regarding government recklessness, overspending, and providing simple, basic accountability for bad decisions? We hear plenty about whistleblowers and quid pro quo when it concerns the actions of President Donald Trump, but where's their reporting on Team Obama's bizarre funding of narcotrafficking, particularly in the proven case of the Honduran government?

Isn't there an important story about government waste being left unreported in El Salvador and Guatemala, where the governments took in $1 billion between them to control refugee migration and yet left it uncontrolled?

There's been extensive media coverage of President Trump's dealing with Northern Triangle region refugees on American soil. Will we see any reporting on Joe Biden's "assistance" for corrupt governments and cocaine cartels back in their countries of origin? Isn't there an investigation needed into how so much money made a problem it was supposed to solve into something substantially worse? By looking at the results, the obvious question is: was *Alliance for Prosperity* meant to face the problem in Central America, or did it become an illusion of pretending to do so?

Because that's all this was. While there are certainly grave safety and security challenges in the Northern Triangle countries, grave enough for tens-of-thousands of residents to desperately flee northward to attempt illegal entry to the United States, Joe Biden's *Alliance for Prosperity* was not really meant for them.

Here's a needed perspective on this from within the Northern Triangle itself:[37]

> *"Biden is taking credit for doing something constructive to stop the migration crisis and blaming the concentration camps [on the US-Mexico border] on Trump. But it's Biden's policies that are driving more people out of Central America and making human rights defenders lives more precarious by defending entities that have no interest in human rights", explained Adrienne Pine, a professor of anthropology at American University and leading researcher of the social crisis in Honduras, in an interview with The Grayzone.*

> *"So $750 million US taxpayer dollars (FY2016) that were allocated to supposedly address child migration are actually making things worse", Pine added. "It started with unaccompanied minors and now you have children in cages. Largely thanks to Biden."*

Obviously, that's not how Team Obama promoted it. Here's their view as expressed in Joe Biden's Office of the Vice President *Blair House Communique* of February 24, 2016.

> *"The presidents of El Salvador, Salvador Sanchez Cerén; Guatemala, Jimmy Morales; and Honduras, Juan Orlando Hernandez; and the Vice President of the United States, Joe Biden, met in Washington,*

DC on February 24, 2016 to review joint efforts to promote economic integration in the Northern Triangle of Central America; to invest in human capital; to provide greater opportunities to all citizens; to ensure more accountable, transparent, and effective public institutions; to guarantee a safe and secure environment for their people, with a particular focus on the underlying conditions driving migration to the United States."[38]

Blah, blah, blah.

Note the timing comes early in the critical election year *after* Team Obama and the Democrats have labeled Donald Trump anti-Hispanic. In my opinion, after looking at all of the personalities involved and the unchecked spending, *Alliance for Prosperity* was a high-dollar pandering to Hispanic voters and nothing but.

The rest of the *Blair House Communique* outlines all the "great" work they've done so far and all the "constructive steps" they'll take going forward. Sorry, but I just can't help but hear *"unindicted co-conspirator"* or *"pled guilty to drug trafficking"* whispered after every sentence.

What about you, Joe? You hearing those whispers?

It's important to understand how this all started. Fast reverse a couple of years and see this transcript I prepared of Joe addressing the press on June 20, 2014, during a trip to Guatemala.[39] At this moment in time the continually rising unaccompanied minor crisis was sending hot whips of panic through the Obama White House.

With the 2014 midterm election looming, Team Obama had to find a cure for this messy humanitarian crisis, and they needed to find it fast. Notice that it isn't until the end that Joe says anything about narcotrafficking:

"I'm going to address the steps we're taking on the immediate crisis in a moment", said Joe. "But in the meantime, here in Central America, I want to talk first about our work together to give citizens in Central America security and -- so that they can thrive -- and not feel the need or be compelled to try to get to the United States of America, or Mexico, for that matter... The United States toward that end provides -- plans to provide 160 million more dollars this year for the Central American Regional Security Initiative to help countries improve citizen safety, governance and border security. The United States will also move forward on projects totaling $83.5 million this year in addition to improve citizen safety in Guatemala, El Salvador, and Honduras. This includes over $40 million over the next several years to Guatemala to target hotspot communities to reduce the risks, the risk factors for youth involved in gangs and drugs.

"I presented today a map to all the leaders showing a direct correlation between the number of unaccompanied minors and where they came from. It directly correlates to the most dangerous cities in Central America. You can just map it. It's clear.

"And so as I said, it's incredibly important that we do our part to provide this kind of funding. And in the case of Guatemala, it's a $40 million additional commitment to target those hot spots to reduce the risk factors for youth involvement in gangs.

"Others are driven to emigrate by lack of economic opportunity. That's been a story. Long before narcotrafficking -- a major problem in Central America, there was still tens of thousands of people over time -- Central America to the United States. So it's not just -- it's not just narcotraffickers and violence."

But it was narcotraffickers, Joe. That's who you entrusted with our tax dollars, the very people who sabotaged the supposed goals the program was aiming for, and instead of stemming the tide of refugees, caused more of the same. That money would have been better spent on something Americans need — like infrastructure.

And don't think our Northern Triangle friends missed the significance of the map Joe presented. Once they understood that the White House was scared out of their socks by the hordes of kids coming out of the "dangerous cities" marked out on that map, they leveraged Team Obama's paltry assistance levels into a foreign aid bonanza to the tune of $1.5 billion dollars.

That trip Joe made to Guatemala in 2014 marked the beginning of a very expensive band-aid for a crisis that now six years later may finally be resolvable. President Trump's combination of responsible administration of foreign aid, pressure on foreign leaders, and the brokering of safe third country repatriation agreements, are producing measurable results on the southern United States border. All of these maneuvers were available six years ago, but considered unworkable (or maybe even impossible) by Barack Obama, the Democrats in Congress, and Joe Biden.

In the beginning, the *Alliance for Prosperity* was publicized by Joe with the same enthusiasm as his solution for Cyprus. The amount of money poured into the Northern Triangle shows how much the United States Congress (on behalf of the U.S. taxpayer) meant for the program to succeed. Joe led the effort, but like Cyprus, both ended the same way, with the situation unchanged *or even worse.*

The tragic lesson is that if Joe (and President Obama) had picked partners not deeply involved in corruption and narcotrafficking, perhaps the *Alliance for Prosperity* could have made a difference. Instead, it made what followed Joe and Barack necessary. Today President Trump is building a wall. It has some logistical challenges, but it does what it's supposed to do and it's *real*.

The Greatest Joe Biden Speech You Never Heard

CHAPTER TEN

I f you want to know someone, truly know them, then understand what they love and listen to them talk about it.

Dick Cheney loves hunting and fishing. George W. Bush loves baseball and Texas. Barack Obama loves Barack Obama. Mike Pence loves his scripture and his Savior. Donald Trump loves greatness and winning.

They all love America.

Ditto for Joe Biden.

He loves America. He loves our Constitution. He loves the United States Senate, and he loves the Democratic Party.

One of best speeches I have ever heard — and I have listened to thousands — was delivered on September 16, 2011, by Joe Biden at the first James R. Soles Lecture on the Constitution and Citizenship at the *University of Delaware,* which is Joe's alma mater.

It is a speech of genius and love, honesty and accomplishment — and if he gave it today, it would devastate his presidential campaign.

Think about that and what it says about our political divisiveness: a speech advocating bipartisan compromise given in 2011 by Vice President Joe Biden is now in 2020 too moderate for him to give as a presidential candidate for the Democratic Party.

Not a joke.

I think political speeches achieve greatness when they crystallize with words what a national audience feels is essential for their future.

On that date, at that point in history, Joe Biden accomplished just that. It was, in my opinion, the closest he ever came to sounding presidential.

The irony is he was speaking to unify a country which was growing ever more divisive — in no small part — through the policies and tactics of the Obama White House and their operatives.

But here was a White House politician actually holding up the mirror about his or her party's shortcomings, and it was remarkable. As Joe likes to joke: *"No one ever doubts I mean what I say; the problem is I sometimes say all that I mean."*

His 2011 James R. Soles[40] lecture is one of those times.

The gathering at the college that evening was small, but Joe's words were meant for all Americans. The audience was certainly composed mostly of his fellow Democrats, but also in attendance were those Americans he optimistically saw as reasonable Republicans and independents.

Typically, since it was Joe's speech and not Barack Obama's, the media ignored it. Unless you were there, this is probably the first time you're hearing about it. This only underscores how infrequently the media is able to accurately judge matters of greatness, quality and importance, and so, yes, I invite you to consider it here for those properties. Not just on the merits of when and why it was given, making it a time capsule of what the Democratic Party used to be, but also who Joe Biden was.

Because in September 2011, it was not so far-fetched for Joe Biden to think he could offer a bipartisan message to a national audience, especially since his core message — and one the tenets of his very existence— was that compromise and consensus within our political system are *essential for America's long-term success.*

It certainly reached me, and still does, even though I'm not a Democrat. That's what's notable about this speech: no reasonable person who cares about America could disagree with it. To me, this speech wasn't about furthering the objectives of the Obama White House, it was about Joe Biden's vision of *our America.*

And I bought into it because Joe rendered it honestly. I could hear that honesty in every word.

With a measured enthusiasm, much like the professor of constitutional law[41] he used to be, he presented his thoughts. He showed his reverence for our Founding Fathers; his statesman's interpretation of the meaning of our Constitution; and his statesman's plea for the ennobling truth that only through compromise will we ensure the continued greatness of our constitutional republic.

So what were Joe's messages from this 2011 time capsule?

First, there's Joe's conviction that compromise is the lifeblood of our political system. He said it because he had lived it.

> *"The true accomplishment of the Founders"*, said Joe, *"was not that they spoke in one voice — but rather that out of many voices they*

forged a compact that has steered our nation safely through more than two centuries of challenge and change, making us the oldest democracy in the world."

The second principle of Joe's speech was when he spoke of the intentional uncertainty the Founders wrote into our Constitution.

That's right, *uncertainty,* as in no one then or even now, 240-plus years later, is really sure how, or if, this republic of ours is going to work out.

"But the Founders also knew that the questions they wrestled with then would not be settled by the words of the Constitution", said Joe, "but could be settled by the institutions to which the Constitution gave rise."

Here he's talking about how our *"indispensable nation"*[42] has evolved out of the principles and institutions written into existence in 1788 by men who could not then even dream of the America we today inhabit.

As much as we pride ourselves on our historical knowledge of our Founding Fathers, we have to admit that we can't fully see their world through their eyes. We don't know with certainty their motivations and influences. At best we have only hints and clues. The best clue they left us is our Constitution.

I love this concept of the institutions over the words because, to me, it's sensible in our modernizing world. It strikes me as the key to accepting our American experiment *as an experiment.* Not a formula, but an experiment. Nothing about our future should be taken for granted. *Ever.*

That's why I think Donald Trump has the one of best summations of our democracy I've ever heard. *"It's all one big, fat, beautiful negotiation",* he said in a wry aside to General Kelly.[43]

Great line, Mr. President. I'd love to return to that later. But for now I have to return to Joe and his Soles lecture because... well, *you'll see.*

Within Biden's discussion of the Founders' use of intentional uncertainty over actual words, Joe outlines an argument for the expectation of privacy, as protected by the Constitution, and unwittingly drops an irony bomb, making a direct hit on Barack Obama's FBI stooges:

> *"But there is an expectation of privacy — is an expectation of privacy — if you're talking on a telephone without probable cause on the part of the government to wiretap that phone."*

That's Joe Biden in 2011 warning against exactly what Team Obama did to Donald Trump's presidential campaign in 2016, which occurred when FBI operatives manufactured "probable cause" to obtain court approval of the kind of wiretaps Joe was warning about!

Irony, anyone? How about treason?

I have to believe every progressive in the land agreed with Joe in 2011, but what about *now* when that warning from just a few years earlier captures the Nixonian paranoia exhibited by Barack Obama's FBI stooges in 2016?

Heaven forbid the Obama-fawning press agree with President Trump about the treasonous investigation waged against his campaign and transition team.

But so far they don't. Maybe that will change when the real truth comes out explaining the duplicity and efforts to cover up these activities.

But, back in 2011, Joe was not done with his prescient warnings. Not by a long shot.

In an even more righteously ironic passage, as he discusses the origins of Jefferson's advocacy for states' rights, Joe quotes George Washington's opinion on the threat of unreasonable partisanship.

Apparently, George Washington understood conspiratorial minds as well as Donald Trump. So, no surprise, the Father of Our Country's quote describes the 2020 version of Joe and his Democrats to a T.

Understand this is Joe of 2011 on George of 1790:

> *"But here's what [Washington] said — he said: while some partisan conflict was inevitable, it must not rise to the level where men 'who oppose the government in all measure are determined by clogging its wheels indirectly to change the nature of it, and in the process to subvert the Constitution.'"*

Resist, cabal, coup — whatever you want to call it, Joe Biden was in 2011 gifting us with George Washington's prescient wisdom that the impeachment the Democrats and their media friends have conjured up is nothing less than "subverting the Constitution".

Wow. One more reason to love George Washington.

Can any Democrat who voted for the impeachment of Donald Trump in the city named after our great first president deny they were acting — in Washington's sage words— "to subvert the Constitution"?

Can they understand the quote their presidential forerunner Joe Biden dredged up (as a warning about his Tea Party adversaries in 2011) now applies *to them?*

Their efforts against the lawfully elected 45th President, Donald Trump, and his supporters will not only prove futile but will put them on the wrong side of history.

George Washington said so.

It's clear that Joe and his modern day Democrats don't see what a growing majority of Americans can see: a drive by that group to seek revenge through impeachment, dividing America for *'partisan conflict'* and invalidating the integrity of their party.

Joe then offered the audience at this first presentation of the James R. Soles Lecture on the Constitution and Citizenship a review of the history of the Civil Rights Act passage of 1964, an effort undertaken by Congress eight years before Joe's election to the Senate as a 29-year-old kid in 1972.

At that time in 1964, Congress was almost entirely comprised of white males, that group regularly accused of being untrustworthy by today's progressive Democrats. But how could anyone, especially today's Democrats, deny that this historic event of the two parties coming together did not ennoble this country?

At least Joe found it ennobling. So do I. So do most reasonable Americans.

Woke or unwoke, ennobling is *ennobling.*

But that prompts the obvious question: how cognizant are progressive Democrats of the fact that it was mostly "old white guys", Democrats and Republicans, who dutifully served *all* their constituents — including their black supporters — and so birthed the 1964 Civil Rights Act into being?

Not very. Not according to the anger they now direct at "old white guys".

As legislators bettering the entire country and correcting a historical wrong, those "old white guys" of 1964 struck a deal despite determined opposition, and by doing so taught their segregationist foes a lesson about the power of being on the *right side of history,* that modern phrase so frequently used by Barack Obama.

I shudder to think how angry our modern Democrats would be to hear Joe's 2011 speech celebrating the passage of the Civil Rights Act, because it contained something that is so ferociously opposed by today's progressives. That special something was what Joe turned to in the last part of his speech as he used his own personal experience to make his point.

Joe now spoke about being in the Senate, where he formed a working relationship with Southern segregationists, many of them fellow Democrats, whom he named without stooping to insult. With them, Joe spoke on how they all worked together upon the important issues of that era to benefit America. In the process, Joe lavished praise on segregationists like Strom Thurmond, Jesse Helms, and John Stennis.

Are there many politicians today who can acknowledge the ugliest elements in their party or the other party, as Joe did, and yet work alongside them for the overall good?

Because both Democrats and Republicans have ugly elements in their political parties. *Both.*

Joe Biden gave what I can't help but call *The Greatest Joe Biden Speech That You Never Heard,*[44] because it contained an essential truth that moved from George Washington, up through American history to the Civil Rights Act of 1964, and right up to now, and Joe Biden put it all together for us to hear that night in Delaware: *bipartisan compromise.*

But what about now, Joe? Is compromise a word any of us can associate with the Democratic Party of 2020?

Could any of the Democratic congresswomen known as *The Squad* even utter the word *compromise*? They've threatened to primary their own Democratic colleagues who are too moderate. *Yikes.*

Is the Democratic Party of 2020 actually proud of the slipshod, one-sided impeachment of President Trump? Not an iota of compromise anywhere near that process. Their effort was so partisan they lost members and supporters who couldn't abide its foolishness

The greatness of the American political system celebrated by Joe in Delaware in 2011 made him, at that moment, also great.

But greatness doesn't last — not in politicians, not in political institutions, and not in political parties.

And not in Joe Biden.

After being heavily criticized for July 2019 speech mentioning his reasonable acceptance of a working relationship in the past with segregationists, Joe found himself up against the "woke" youngsters of his party. The theme of bipartisan compromise was one he had lived with all of his political life, but now Joe caved in and issued an apology.

> *"Now, was I wrong a few weeks ago to somehow give the impression to people that I was praising those men who I successfully opposed time and again?" he said to a largely black audience in South Carolina. "Yes, I was. I regret it. I'm sorry for any of the pain and misconception I may have caused anybody."*[45]

That, more than anything, reveals the awful truth of what he and his Democratic Party have transformed themselves into during the Trump era: ineffective, divisive, and intolerant.

Joe can repackage the truth, but he can't hide from it. That description matches him as well. Like his party, he has changed, changed utterly, and it has not been beautiful.

Joe Biden used to talk about the presidency of Barack Obama as an inflection point in American history, the point at which everything changed for the better.

He's campaigning on it now as though that "marvelous" era is only a small comeback victory away.

As an eyewitness to history from inside three consecutive presidencies, I argue that Joe Biden's September 2011 speech is the real inflection point, that is to say that point at which everything changed — changed utterly — especially for Joe.

Joe's speech was the last best gasp before his party embraced intolerance and divisiveness over compromise and consensus.

I worked for Team Obama in their White House. I heard what they said. I saw what they did. They are co-creators of our divided country. For me to say anything less is a lie.

The day after Joe Biden delivered that speech praising the American history of bipartisan compromise, Occupy Wall Street moved into Zuccotti Park. Soon after Team Obama directed their unrelenting scorn at "millionaires and billionaires", thus bringing forth the populist wing of the modern Democratic Party.

Hear all that screaming for socialism? That's them.

The antagonistic and divisive "old white guy" stuff followed soon after.

Seriously, what has *happened* to that party?.

Talk about an *inflection point.*

There are a lot of reasonable people in our country now who are not sure where that party is headed. But they are dead certain that anything any Democratic leader says at this point in history is a danger to their future and an insult to their past.

The Joe Biden who spoke so eloquently of compromise and consensus in 2011 cannot help them. He is gone. In his place is an "old white guy" Democrat pointing his finger at the "old white guy" Republicans and cheering the impeachment of their lawfully elected president, not realizing how his subversion of the Constitution is about to backfire on him and his intolerant party.

Trapped

CHAPTER ELEVEN

J oe Biden walked into a trap.

It happened this way: there is a video of an weak old man who doesn't understand how weak and old he is. *His name is Joe Biden.*

In the video, he is sitting next to an angry, resolute man who understands exactly how resolute and angry he is. *His name is Recep Tayyip Erdogan.*

I have never seen this video. I don't have to. I was an eyewitness to the proceedings and stood mere feet from the videocameras recording it, so I am certain of its creation, and I assume, continued existence.

As this is my memoir, I am offering this description based on my recollection of being there and seeing what I saw, and since I am certain no one on Team Biden can contradict me without *also* obtaining and releasing the video, I suspect you'll just have to take my word for what happened.

I guarantee Joe Biden — because he is Joe Biden — does not think he walked into a trap, just as he does not think he looked weak and old as he spoke with Erdogan.

But I do — and, aye, there's the rub — there's that video to back me up.

But if it could exonerate Joe, it has to be first released to the public to view and decide.

How that occurs, if it ever happens, will be a story unto itself, as you'll learn as this alarming episode unfolds.

What I saw August 24, 2016, at the meeting between the Vice President of the United States and the Leader of Turkey was the stark contrast of a weak old man next to an angry, resolute man. I once described the scene to a friend as there were two men in a room — one was a lamb and one was a lion. Our guy was the *lamb*.

Now, consider that if I hadn't written here about the video documentation and its significance in showing the entrapment of Joe Biden. You would never know of its existence and the important evidence it captured, how it shows the abilities of a determined, but very tired, aged and completely outmatched senior leader of the U.S. government unable to perform his official duties up against a powerful foreign leader. Without my witness of that event, you would not know about this.

Never as in *not ever.*

But wait, journalists were there, right? Yes, journalists were there. They saw what happened.

Thank goodness, *the day is saved!* The truth will come out! Because we know *we can trust journalists!*

Well, anyway, *yes,* there were independent print reporters and still photographers present, American and Turkish, but no *independent videographers.*

Which is critical because in modern news gathering, video shows the totality of the event — not just slivers of it.

Notably, the videographers there were Turkish and *only Turkish*. No Biden videographer, no American videographer. And they were Erdogan's house videographers. He controlled them. Not journalists, not independent videographers, but Erdogan videographers following orders.

That part of the trap was essential because it was one of the reasons the Turks choreographed Joe's visit and movements, manipulating him into being privately recorded as the lamb next to their lion.

And for me, that's the scariest part of what happened.

First, the context: August 24, 2016, was a month after rogue factions of the Turkish army led a coup[46] against President Erdogan's government with tanks, attack helicopters, and fighter jets.

(This was a busy week for more people than just Erdogan and Joe, though. This was also about the time when Donald Trump fired his second of three campaign managers in an amazing, full throttle march to the presidency. While Joe was being exploited by Erdogan like a lamb, a different American was behaving like a lion.)

The attempted coup cast Turkey into a dark period. Years later it is still confronting the consequences of the coup attempt where legislators lost their lives in an attack on their parliament. Hundreds of everyday citizens were killed in their weaponless fight against tanks, attack helicopters, and fighter jets. Thousands of soldiers died at the hands of their rebellious colleagues.

But democracy — Erdogan's version of it, at least — prevailed.

Team Obama's slow response to the coup infuriated the Turks, especially

Erdogan. Team Erdogan was further angered by Obama's unwillingness to immediately extradite the man Erdogan blamed for the attack, Fethullah Gülen,[47] who was living in a compound in Saylorsburg, Pennsylvania.

But on the Air Force Two flight into Ankara, the Turkish capital, the discussion was more about Team Obama's concern that their already inadequate war on ISIS, highly dependent upon cooperation from allies in the region, was taking a turn for the worse as the Turks had begun shelling the Kurds in Syria. *"It's never good when one ally is shelling another ally"*, sighed one VP staffer.

So we faced obvious and serious diplomatic tension as we flew into the Ankara airport, and yet Joe and his staff had not prepared for what could be waiting for us on arrival. The Vice President was officially greeted at the airport by Ankara's deputy mayor, a move so minimally lacking in red carpet treatment it stank of disrespect.

This insult, though, was just the softening up phase.

Next was Turkish Speaker of Parliament Ismail Kahraman, without Erdogan in sight, walking Joe through room after room of destruction in the bombed-out Turkish parliament.

A horde of press followed at Joe's heels, in his favorite theatrical scene — he, as the American political celebrity, mobbed by the press who hung on every word and gesture. Still photographers, videographers, pen and ink scribblers, the three members of the White House press pool who were traveling on Air Force Two — they were all there, rushing, scrambling, crowding up against the security teams to apprise themselves of Joe's dramatic tour amidst the rubble.

At one point Joe mustered his grimmest demeanor and said, *"This is devastating, can you imagine if this happened at home?"*

Joe was off next to meet with Prime Minister Binali Yildirim at Cankaya Palace.

But still no Erdogan.

After their meeting, Biden and Yildirim met the press for limited questions, which was televised live to a global audience, another perfect setup for Joe.

Clearly, this was the *buttering up* phase.

Joe, now in front of a large world audience, showed that he was conflicted about the destruction he'd just seen. Energized, he addressed the coup, Team Obama's tepid response to it, plus Team Obama's concerns about the tensions between the U.S., the Turks, and the Kurds as all three were official allies in the fight against ISIS. At one point, he confesses to feeling guilty about the lack of urgency in scheduling the visit, a good touch in a good performance for both the Turkish and American audiences.[48]

So this was *Fighter Joe,* definitely not behaving like a lamb, but he's also not yet in the lion's den.

The time was finally right for the main event, and so after a long, hard day of travel, meetings, and endless media attention, Joe is ushered to Erdogan's sprawling 3.2 million square foot Presidential Palace[49] for the final, big meeting of the day.

Welcome to the lion's den.

Upon arrival at the ultramodern government complex, the Turks first pointed to the baseball-sized bullet holes in the floor to ceiling glass windows, then they demonstrated the flight path the attack helicopters took as they strafed the building.

As we stood there, it was haunting how easily the bad guys had pulled that off. Even after seeing the destruction at the Turkish parliament, it was shocking to see such ruthlessness waged against a democratically elected president in his sanctuary.

So, in that sobering atmosphere, Biden and Erdogan and a handful of senior staffers proceeded to an upstairs private room, while the rest of us remained with the press contingent downstairs amid the bullet-riddled rooms, and we waited, and we waited.

And *we waited.*

What was supposed to be a relatively short meeting, followed by a presentation of the two leaders side-by-side for the media pool, was delayed without explanation. The longer the waiting dragged on, the more it felt like a cancellation of further media presentations was in the offing.

We didn't know it at the time, but Erdogan was deploying the oldest trick in the book against Joe — seduction.

Putin humiliated Joe with an appeal to his ego. The Chinese humiliated Joe with surprise brutality. Erdogan did them one better and trapped Joe by playing hard to get with something he desperately needed — a congenial side-by-side in front of the media.

And then suddenly Erdogan relented, the lion gave a knowing nod, the press were given the green light. Biden staffers were ebullient at their "success". We in the press contingent rushed upstairs into the inner sanctum of the lion's lair to see what the two old "friends" had to say.

If it is ever made public, this videotape will show the two men in elegant armchairs, in an elegant room dignified with flags and flowers, but the two are anything but friends. Erdogan's stoic demeanor belies his fury. Biden's squirming demeanor belies his guilt, hence his weakness.

Video viewers will see Biden and Erdogan facing the press for statements and brief questions. Sitting in his chair, Erdogan is as tense as a lion ready to pounce. He barely makes eye contact. Joe Biden, meanwhile, is offering apologies, excuses, and rambling explanations.

Weak.

Cyprus is mentioned in a tone that makes it clear Joe's big connect with Erdogan has already soured.

Three American reporters are in the room — Carol Lee, then of *The Wall Street Journal,* Karen DeYoung of *The Washington Post,* and Justin Sink of *Bloomberg News.* I am standing with them, recording for the transcript.[50]

In politics, image is everything. It's the one area that major politicians and celebrities protect with tenacity, and if necessary, ferocity. When you see that video you will understand Joe Biden surrendered control of his image to Recep Erdogan.

Baaaad move, Joe.

No president I have worked for would ever surrender control of their image to anyone. That's how they rise to the presidency, by covering all the angles.

We flew into Ankara knowing the Turks were enraged, indeed that was the reason for the trip, and still Joe strode right into the trap they laid for him. Joe Biden was too careless to cover all the angles, and so ... well, I'll let you finish the thought.

The story on that meeting that Karen DeYoung wrote for *The Washington Post* was professional and focused largely on the Turkish-Kurdish issue. I wouldn't say it was inaccurate, but she certainly ignored the unflattering aspect of Joe's squirmy apology-fest.

Earlier in the day, as I was helping her load some luggage in our motorcade van, she unexpectedly commented to me about how horrible it would be if Donald Trump became president. I didn't reply because I was already positive Trump would win. So I just changed the topic and noted yet another reporter with anti-Trump bias.

Carol Lee's story for *The Wall Street Journal* was somewhat reflective of what I saw, though muted. Hard to say if that was her or the editing. Carol is one journalist whom I've always trusted as being unbiased.

Justin Sink is another journalist I trust as being unbiased, and his *Bloomberg* reporting was tough and true on Biden's squirmy fumbling with Erdogan. So much so that the next morning in Copenhagen, I complimented him on the accuracy of his story.

"Yeah, but now they'll be mad at me for the rest of the trip", is what I remember him replying.

All three of these reporters' stories — and those of many others who reported on that visit — are available on the internet.

And then there's my assessment here of the lion and the lamb and that videotape. Compared to the reporting by the professional journalists I may seem harsh and overly critical.

But I defy any reporter to see Joe as I did and do.

I saw him bitch-slapped in Moscow. I saw him oblivious to his staff being manhandled in Beijing. I listened to him brag about his exploits in Ukraine — the heroic acts and the corrupt acts. I saw his carelessness with taxpayer funds as he chased diplomatic windmills in Cyprus and funded drug dealers in Central America. I saw the tragic catastrophe of his mismanagement of Iraq.

I don't need the media to inform me about Joe Biden. I know him, better than they. I know his genius and his egotistical carelessness. That is why I knew that in Ankara, Joe the Lamb was getting played, yet again, by Erdogan the Lion.

But in a final twist of irony in this story of the United States and its ally Turkey, the person with the final say on the egotistical carelessness of Joe Biden is none other than President Donald Trump.

Not because of something Trump said, but because of something he showed us. If Recep Tayyip Erdogan is a lion, then Donald Trump is a lion tamer, and one of the best I've ever seen.

Look no farther for proof than the Trump-Erdogan press presentation at the White House in November 2019.

Donald Trump mastered the room. Erdogan was his well-behaved guest. They were businessmen discussing pending deals. Erdogan reiterated his request to have Gülen extradited to Turkey. Trump was noncommittal. No apology offered or needed by either side. It was deal making, pure and simple.

But if Joe Biden is ever actually running against Trump for the presidency, just go to that videotape, because it gives the definitive view of Trump's presidential superiority over Biden. Compare the Trump-Erdogan meeting of 2019 and its image of two leaders talking together against the Biden-Erdogan video of 2016, one man rattled and searching for words while the other sits angrily in control of them both. And that video evidence, which I strongly suspect to appear in the near future, either because a Democratic competitor or a Republican agent will meet the price Erdogan could set for the humiliating spectacle, is where you'll be able to see what I saw so clearly in 2016.

My Word as a Biden

CHAPTER TWELVE

J oe Biden is not just a politician — he's a son, a brother, a husband, a father, an uncle, and a grandfather.

Daily phone calls, motorcade rides, Air Force Two journeys to faraway lands, sleepovers at NavObs, receptions at the White House, inaugural balls — Joe Biden kept his beloved family as close to him as the clothes on his back.

As Vice President, most of his weekends were at his home in quiet Wilmington, amongst family and friends.

Usually, he traveled between Washington and Delaware by train. As a senator, the daily train commute was epic — two hours down, two hours up. The tally for his career: over 2 million miles. Joe Biden did that to be with his family.

In fact, he and his family rode the Amtrak to the 2008 inauguration ceremony with Barack Obama and his family, initiating a bond between the families of the president and vice president unmatched in American history.

Family — *first and foremost.*

That's not always easy. Every year on December 18th, the anniversary of the car accident that took the lives of his first wife, Neilia, and daughter Naomi, is a day of family mourning and remembrance in Wilmington. Joe conducts no official business.

As life events go, that is one of Joe Biden's biggest. He's helped people because of it and hurt people because of it. Mostly helped.

The ugliness of our national politics is that untruths told about our political leaders rise to the common discourse. One such untruth concerns the extra (and as my wife can attest, sometimes unwelcome) attention Joe pays to women and girls.

No doubt Joe Biden is a grabber and a hugger. It's something easily seen in the massive media coverage that has showcased his life over his decades of working in Washington D.C.

But, as someone who has spent endless hours documenting his speeches in person, I've never seen him, or heard of it from the people around him, that Joe ever did anything unwarranted or aggressive with his touching.

Never. *Not once.*

No, to me, there's a grandfatherly wistfulness to a lot of Joe's interactions with women and girls, and I think it has to do with that terrible day in 1972.

Joe is a rock of a husband, always has been. Truth be told, he's been better at it than me. But I think the criticism of him overdoing his greetings with young women is overblown. Yes, he's enthusiastic, welcoming, and informal. If that's as far as it goes, *so what?*

But there's a deeper aspect to it. I see his exuberance as a special way of cherishing that young woman or girl. It's as if they remind him of someone he might have known but didn't. It's as if knowing what loss is, he's trying to hold onto a moment of what his daughter might have been, or his wife might have been by seeing it in someone else.

For that reason, I've never seen Joe Biden do anything creepy with women or girls. I've occasionally been creeped out *by what he says*,[51] but never what he did. There's a difference.

So, to know Joe Biden is to know he weaves his family experiences into every aspect of his life — especially his politics.

He would bring up his parents just about every speech, at which time he would refer to himself by the childhood name his parents used — *Joey*.

"Joey" talks about his mom and dad and what he learned in their generous household, then he'd pass a lesson on to the audience. Safe to say there isn't a speechwriter in the world who can communicate authenticity better than Joe Biden.

"Children become what you expect of them", is one nugget of wisdom passed on by his mother. It's certainly made a difference in my life.

"You are defined by your courage and redeemed by your loyalty", is another from Catherine Eugenia Finnegan Biden.

On many occasions he noted something his mother said that infuriated him as he grieved his deceased wife and baby daughter. *"Joey, out of everything terrible that happens to you, something good will come if you look hard enough for it"*, she said.

Enraged at the time, he's come to admit that, that too, is a keeper.

In Joe's telling his father was heroic for the actions he took: keeping his promises to Joe's grandfather Ambrose Finnegan that he'd be *"back for Jean and the kids"* when he found work in Wilmington; quitting a critical job at an automobile dealership because the owner demeaned his employees at a Christmas party; explaining to his teenage son Joey that the kiss he saw two men share in Rodney Square circa 1958 simply meant that they loved each other.

He identified his father as a righteous Christian and early supporter of Israel, and segued that into explaining his lifelong support for Israel and its people, which was a much tougher sell at the end of the Obama administration than at the beginning.

He used the shame his father expressed at not getting a college loan for Joe as the impetus to craft his first legislation in the Senate: a bill that lowered the threshold for middle-class families to qualify for college loans.

But it was his salesman father's advice on the art of deal making that impressed me most. *"Never back a guy into a corner, Joey"*, he said, *"because he'll come right over top of you to get out"*.

Wise words in the age of Trump.

And family also factored into why the D.C.-based media has been overly lenient with Joe. And while it's not a closely held secret, they certainly don't broadcast it either.

Since the beginning of his vice presidency, Joe Biden has had a devilishly simple plan to stay on the D.C. media's good side. Every year in mid-June, he and his family would invite the Washington media A-listers — and only them — to the *Biden Boardwalk Bash* at the Vice President's Residence.

Don't be surprised if you've never heard of it, that was the idea. The Bidens set it up as a privileged event, and the press attendees were only too happy to cooperate.

I never went. I knew about it from the Vice President's schedule and the photos in the Vice President's hallway in the West Wing.

Basically it was a pool party in which the children of the media guests got into a massive water gun battle with the Vice President of the United States and his family at his backyard pool.

Therefore, it had all the elements of an extra-special Washington day for the press that, of course, had to be kept on the down-low. It was exclusive, yet casual. It was high-profile access, yet wrapped up with family memories. It was the D.C. media glitterati connecting their families heart-to-heart with the Bidens.

Biased media, special times.

Ever wonder why the press gives Joe Biden far more latitude than he deserves? Now you know. As Joe used to say, you do something for my kids, I'm in your debt forever.

Family — first and foremost.

One of the best speeches Joe ever gave was at the Yale University Class Day on May 17, 2015. He was funny. He was witty. He was gracious. He thanked his staffers. He acknowledged the granddaughter of his dear friend Congressman Tom Lantos. He got a laugh quoting his granddaughter Finnegan who had accompanied him. He bragged a bit. Why not? He had Yalies working for him.

But then when he talked about his bond with his sons, Hunter and Beau, he dug out the real Joe and shared a personal truth that he was only then uncovering:

"But looking back on it", he explained, *"the truth be told, the real reason I went home every night was that I needed my children more than they needed me. Some at the time wrote and suggested that Biden can't be a serious national figure. If he was, he'd stay in Washington more, attend to more important events...But I realized I didn't miss a thing. Ambition is really important. You need it. And I certainly have never lacked in having ambition. But ambition without perspective can be a killer."*[52]

Family — first and foremost.

What's really amazing about that speech is how publicly brave Joe was in giving it because at the time he was privately readying himself and his family for the passing of his beloved son Beau, who died 13 days later.

We have a lot of heroes in our lives — heroes in sports, heroes in the arts, heroes of conscience and service, heroes of business, heroes of wars — seen and unseen.

For many Americans, our presidents and first ladies occupy that role for us. I was fortunate to have personally served in the White House for three consecutive presidents and first ladies. I saw their heroism day in and day out. Each couple in their own way.

Nor are they the only heroes in the White House.

From the vice president on down, there are an amazing number of heroes supporting those presidents and their families, working all manner of tasks.

This assemblage of excellence, of dedication, of courage, of character is why people all over the world marvel at the White House and what it represents.

For a span of fifteen years it was my privilege to work for and amongst those Americans — too many to count. I met great people doing great things, literally making history with their heroism.

But I have never, ever witnessed a more moving example of bravery and heroism, of humanity and selflessness than when Joe Biden and his family said goodbye to Beau Biden.

Nothing comes close.

I wasn't there. But a colleague who was summed up that day in two very emotional words, *"Eight hours"*, he said, his voice breaking. *"They stood for eight hours."*

And then he and I hugged because we had to. Those of us who had traveled with Joe Biden, laughed with him, been exasperated by him, toiled for him, felt worse than awful for him. Those of us who could hug him did. Those of us who couldn't, we hugged each other.

Death brings clarity to what at the end of it all is necessary. For the Vice President and his family what was necessary was saying goodbye to Beau Biden with all the love, dignity, and grace they could muster.

President Obama's eulogy was pitch perfect. The ceremony was comforting. The receiving line was the biggest tribute.

Eight hours. The Bidens greeted mourner after mourner — sharing, hugging, appreciating, thanking. Words can't describe.

Eight hours. For a son, a brother, a husband, a father, a nephew, an uncle, a cousin — a great man, gone to soon, mourned by millions.

Joe Biden taught me a lot about life. I'd be lying to say he didn't. I have never witnessed such fatherly heroism as he displayed that day. Eight hours has a whole new meaning for me.

And then in the ensuing months, battling through his grief, honoring his deceased son, ignoring his personal ambition for the presidency, Joe Biden went to work.

And so did we.

Joe's year-long efforts for the *Cancer Moonshot*[53] were monumental. No one should disregard the progress he made to end cancer on behalf of his son Beau.

His staffers were right there with him — long days and weekends in the office, plus a lot of travel with his global outreach. Time with my own family slipped away. But when a dear friend was battling stage four breast cancer, it stopped being a job and became a cause.

I was in Joe's corner the entire time. Never not once did I disagree with what he was trying to do.

Personally, I think he'd be more heroic resuming his *Cancer Moonshot* than campaigning for president. The world needs Joe Biden doing something Joe Bidenish. He's a larger than life American fighter.

Go back to fighting cancer, Joe. Everyone in the world will be in your corner. You'd be doing it for your family and families all around the world. You will win that fight. No way you would lose.

Winning

AFTERWARD

When I started this book in July, 2019, I thought I was writing a cautionary portrait of Joe Biden's dangerous carelessness. But along the way, I realized that dangerous carelessness has infected the Democratic Party as a whole.

They have been incoherent in their constant and unreasonable criticisms of President Trump's accomplishments — both domestic and international — and dangerously willing to degrade him no matter the cost to them or our democratic republic.

And so I end where I began: As the election of 2020 unfolds, I can see that, like the debacle in Turkey in 2016, Joe Biden is walking into a trap, and the Democratic Party is close behind him.

Reasonable American voters will not be kind to either.

Simply put, Joe Biden is no match for Trump when it comes to the matter of presidential effectiveness. And not just Trump compared to Biden, I do not believe there is a Democratic politician alive who could have handled Erdogan like President Trump has done in the wake of Team Obama's 2016 fumble.

Ditto for Trump's handling of Russia, China, Iran, North Korea, the

Northern Triangle countries, Mexico, Canada, et cetera, et cetera.

And that, after all, is the point that has to be made in an election year like 2020.

In the deadly world of international politics, lions eat lambs.

All the time.

If you're a Joe Biden believer, or fundraiser, or volunteer, I wish you could see the undoctored, unedited video of that event in Ankara I discussed in Chapter Nine. I guarantee it will give you some clarity and save us all a lot of time and money.

But the truth is that it never should have happened that way in Turkey. It didn't have to. The same for what happened in Ukraine with Hunter Biden's activities at Burisma Holdings, or the disaster in the Northern Triangle with American money being pumped into the hands of drug traffickers. No one set out to make corruption prosper, but that's what happened.

The effort, time and money put into the Russian "reset", solving the Cyprus stalemate, these initiatives came with high hopes attached, and then suddenly there was nothing to show for it, nothing that looked anything like an improvement, or even *a discernible change.*

Having American prestige bullied in China was a hard pill to swallow, but far worse, the "solving" of Iraq that only produced eight more years of atrocity and bloodshed.

We American voters want our president to succeed, of course, and we're willing to tolerate failure if it will lead to success later. But failure reproducing more failure is not winning.

Which brings me to Donald Trump.

Since 2016, under a relentless assault in the media and from the Democratic Party, President Trump has nonetheless managed to pull rabbit-after-rabbit out of a hat, doing what experts proclaimed was impossible in 2016: super low unemployment, bolstered manufacturing jobs, expanding investment and infrastructure, a record-breaking Wall Street, real pressure on China to fix unfair trade practices, investment into military preparedness not seen since Reagan, and improved foreign relations in places that had long stagnated.

Record-against-record, that's how reasonable Americans pick our presidents. It's always been that way. Even with all that's been stacked against him in his first term, Donald Trump will win his second term and go down in history as one of our greatest presidents. Ever.

Joe Biden is a great American. He will never be president.

Appendix I

A Timeline of Joe and Hunter Biden's Sketchy Business

1   June 2009, Hunter Biden, Devon Archer, and Chris Heinz form Rosemont Seneca Partners, https://www.nationalreview.com/2019/09/hunter-biden-comprehensive-timeline/

2   July 2009, Vice President Joe Biden travels to Kyiv, Ukraine, announces Obama administration working group for Ukrainian energy security to counter Russian coercion, https://obamawhitehouse.archives.gov/the-press-office/remarks-vice-president-biden-ukraine

3   March 2010, Mykola Zlochevsky, founder/owner of Cyprus-based Brociti Investments Limited, which in turn owns Burisma Holdings, Ukraine's largest private natural gas company, named Ukrainian Minister for Ecology and Natural Resources, https://www.foxbusiness.com/money/what-you-need-to-know-about-the-ukrainian-gas-company-at-the-center-of-hunter-biden-controversy

4   March 2010, Hunter Biden ends seven years of 12-step sobriety with a vodka binge; 2013, Hunter Biden relapses after another unsuccessful rehab attempt, https://www.newyorker.com/magazine/2019/07/08/will-hunter-biden-jeopardize-his-fathers-campaign

5   May 2013, Hunter Biden reports to United States Navy Reserve, Norfolk, Virginia, intake drug test yields positive for cocaine, https://www.newyorker.com/magazine/2019/07/08/will-hunter-biden-jeopardize-his-fathers-campaign

6   December 2013, Vice President Joe Biden travels to Japan, China, and South Korea, Hunter Biden accompanies and allegedly conducts personal business in Beijing on behalf of Rosemont Seneca Partners, https://obamawhitehouse.archives.gov/photos-and-video/photo/2013/12/vice-president-joe-biden-granddaughter-finnegan

7   December 2013, Pro-democracy demonstrators fortify and occupy Maidan Square in Kyiv, Ukraine, https://www.youtube.com/watch?v=O8wbp4ngd0c

8   January 2014, Zlochevsky, seeks to "westernize" Burisma Holdings with international board members, names former Polish President Aleksander Kwasniewski to the board, https://polandin.com/44767911/former-polish-president-and-the-ukrainian-investigation-into-biden

9   February 19, 2014, Navy Reserve officially discharges Hunter Biden for positive cocaine result, no official announcement, https://www.washingtontimes.com/news/2019/dec/30/hunter-biden-file-brief-navy-career/

10 February 20, 2014, Vice President Joe Biden successfully admonishes Ukrainian President Viktor Yanukovych to halt the sniper massacre of Maidan pro-democracy demonstrators, saving hundreds of Ukrainian protesters, https://obamawhitehouse.archives.gov/the-press-office/2014/02/20/readout-vice-president-bidens-call-ukrainian-president-viktor-yanukovych

11 February 21, 2014, Viktor Yanukovych flees Ukraine, pro-democracy reforms sweep the country, https://obamawhitehouse.archives.gov/the-press-office/2014/02/21/statement-press-secretary-ukraine

12   March 2014, Vladimir Putin launches "green men" invasion of Ukraine, https://www.youtube.com/watch?v=TNKsLlK52ss

13   March 11, 2014, Zlochevsky is thwarted attempting to transfer $23 million of Burisma Holdings' cash from BNP Paribas in London to Cyprus, the United Kingdom's Serious Fraud Office opens a money laundering investigation, freezing Burisma Holdings' assets, https://www.theguardian.com/world/2017/apr/12/the-money-machine-how-a-high-profile-corruption-investigation-fell-apart

14   March 18, 2014, Vice President Joe Biden travels to Poland and Lithuania to reassure the region the Obama administration will stand up to Putin; Biden, now Team Obama's point man on Ukraine, begins planning a relief trip to Ukraine to include substantial assistance for energy security, possible contact with Kwasniewski, https://obamawhitehouse.archives.gov/the-press-office/2014/03/18/remarks-press-vice-president-joe-biden-president-bronislaw-komorowski-po

15   March/April 2014, Kwasniewski recruits Hunter Biden as Burisma Holdings board member; Zlochevsky decamps to Cyprus to flee legal difficulties in Ukraine and advises Kwasniewski to recruit Devon Archer to the Burisma board, https://www.newyorker.com/magazine/2019/07/08/will-hunter-biden-jeopardize-his-fathers-campaign

16.   April 14, 2014, London judge freezes all U.K.-held assets of Brociti and Burisma, https://www.theguardian.com/world/2017/apr/12/the-money-machine-how-a-high-profile-corruption-investigation-fell-apart

17   April 15, 2014, 11:30 a.m., Devon Archer makes a WAVES appointment for a meeting with Vice President Joe Biden for the following day; 12:00 p.m., Biden departs the White House with a full staff contingent to speak at the Boston Marathon Bombing Commemoration; 4:30 p.m.,

President Barack Obama convenes a meeting in the Roosevelt Room with his "brain trust", David Axelrod, David Plouffe, and Jim Messina, specifically excluding Biden, see 2014 WAVES spreadsheet, Figure 2.

18. April 16, 2014, 7:30 a.m., David Axelrod transports to the Vice President's Residence for breakfast with Vice President Joe Biden and possibly Hunter Biden; 11:30 a.m., Devon Archer meets with Joe Biden and possibly Hunter Biden in the West Wing, see 2014 WAVES spreadsheet, Figure 3 & 4

19 April 18, 2014, Hunter Biden and Devon Archer are surreptitiously named to the board of Burisma Holdings, no public announcement but compensation is initiated, https://www.nationalreview.com/2020/01/trump-impeachment-hunter-biden-connection-to-burisma-questioned-before/

20 April 21-22, Vice President Joe Biden travels to Ukraine with billion dollar loan guarantees and substantial assistance for energy security, specifically the natural gas sector, publicly promises phone calls to Hungary, Slovakia, and Poland to discuss further investments in Ukrainian natural gas sector, possible phone contact with Burisma board member Kwasniewski, https://obamawhitehouse.archives.gov/the-press-office/2014/04/22/remarks-press-vice-president-joe-biden-and-ukrainian-prime-minister-arse

21 May 13, 2014, Burisma Holdings puts out a press release acknowledging that Hunter Biden and Devon Archer have joined their board; then and *only then* does Chris Heinz learn of his business partners ties to Burisma and he immediately severs the relationship. A spokeswoman for Vice President Biden denies there is a conflict of interest, stating that Vice President Biden "has no involvement with this company", https://www.washingtonexaminer.com/politics/john-kerrys-son-cut-business-ties-with-hunter-biden-over-ukrainian-oil-deal

22   May 22, 2014, Vice President Joe Biden travels to Romania and Cyprus, speaks on situation in Ukraine, plus Cyprus unification talks, possible contact with Zlochevsky in Cyprus, https://obamawhitehouse.archives. gov/the-press-office/2014/05/12/vice-president-biden-and-dr-jill-biden-travel-romania-and-cyprus

23   June 7, 2014, Vice President Joe Biden travels to Kyiv, Ukraine for inauguration of newly elected President Petro Poroshenko, possible contact with Kwasniewski who is also in attendance, https://www.kyivpost. com/article/content/eu-ukraine-relations/kwasniewski-sees-ukraines-readiness-for-dialogue-with-russia-351030.html

24. October 2014, Hunter Biden publicly acknowledges his discharge from the Navy Reserve, https://www.wsj.com/articles/bidens-son-hunter-discharged-from-navy-reserve-after-failing-cocaine-test-1413499657-test-1413499657

25   November 2014, Vice President Joe Biden travels to Kyiv, Ukraine, declares he has never talked to his son Hunter about his business when questioned by a reporter, https://obamawhitehouse.archives.gov/the-press-office/2014/11/21/background-briefing-senior-administration-officials-trip-vice-president-

25   January 21, 2015, London judge lifts freeze order on Burisma and Brociti's U.K.-held assets, criticizes Ukrainian Prosecutor General's Office for mishandling evidence; $23 million is eventually transferred to Cyprus, https://www.theguardian.com/world/2017/apr/12/the-money-machine-how-a-high-profile-corruption-investigation-fell-apart

26   May 2015, Beau Biden dies of glioblastoma, https://www.theguardian. com/us-news/2015/may/31/beau-biden-dies-of-brain-cancer

27 Summer 2015, CIA Director Brennan assigns CIA analyst Eric Ciara-
    mella to White House National Security Council to assist Vice Presi-
    dent Biden with Ukraine policy, https://www.realclearinvestigations.
    com/articles/2019/10/30whistleblower_exposed_close_to_biden_bren-
    nan_dnc_oppo_researcher_120996.html

28 July 2015, Kathleen Biden kicks Hunter Biden out of their home
    after 22 years of marriage, https://www.dailymail.co.uk/news/arti-
    cle-4276134/Kathleen-Biden-divorce-docs-reveal-kicked-Hunter.html

29 October 2015, Hunter Biden separates from Kathleen Biden, https://
    www.dailymail.co.uk/news/article-4276134/Kathleen-Biden-divorce-
    docs-reveal-kicked-Hunter.html

30 December 2015, Vice President Joe Biden returns to Ukraine, com-
    plains about corruption in Prosecutor General Viktor Shokin's Office,
    hands over $1 billion in aid after contentious meeting with Ukrainian
    government officials, https://obamawhitehouse.archives.gov/the-press-
    office/2015/12/07/remarks-vice-president-joe-biden-and-ukrainian-
    president-petro

31 March 2016, Ukraine Prosecutor General Viktor Shokin is fired by
    President Poroshenko, https://www.independent.co.uk/news/world/
    europe/viktor-shokin-ukraine-prosecutor-trump-biden-hunter-joe-
    investigation-impeachment-a9147001.html

32 May 11, 2016, the Securities Exchange Commission charges Devon Ar-
    cher for participating in defrauding investors in sham Native American
    tribal bonds; June 2018, he is convicted in a jury trial; November 2018,
    the conviction is overturned, https://www.sec.gov/litigation/litreleas-
    es/2016/lr23535.htm

33   August 2016, Vice President Joe Biden boasts of withholding $1 billion in aid to force Ukraine President Poroshenko to fire Prosecutor General Viktor Shokin during an interview with Steve Clemons of *The Atlantic,* does not acknowledge that Shokin was allegedly investigating Burisma Holdings, https://www.theatlantic.com/international/archive/2016/08/biden-doctrine/496841/

34   November 8, 2016, Donald Trump is elected President of the United States

35   December 2016, Kathleen Biden files for divorce from Hunter Biden, https://www.dailymail.co.uk/news/article-4276134/Kathleen-Biden-divorce-docs-reveal-kicked-Hunter.html

36   January 2017, Joe Biden travels to Ukraine for the final time as Vice President

37   January 20, 2017, Donald Trump is inaugurated as the 45th President of the United States

38   April 2017, Kathleen Biden at a hearing finalizing her divorce from Hunter Biden details he indulged in "drugs, alcohol, prostitutes, strip clubs and gifts for women with whom he had sexual relations"; Hunter Biden, who is not in court, is at the time dating his dead brother's widow, https://www.dailymail.co.uk/news/article-4276134/Kathleen-Biden-divorce-docs-reveal-kicked-Hunter.html

Appendix II

A Timeline of Joe Biden's Life

1942 – Joseph Robinette Biden, Jr. is born November 20, in Scranton, Pennsylvania to Catherine Eugenia Biden (maiden name: Finnegan) and Joseph Robinette Biden, Sr.

Joseph Biden will be the oldest of four children. In reflection on his childhood and community environment in 2008, Biden said that the reason he does not consume alcohol is *"...there are enough alcoholics in my family."* (NY Times, Oct. 23, 2008)

1947 – Begins kindergarten and goes to Marywood College to meet with a speech specialist to deal with a stutter (later in life he will use poetry recitation in private to overcome the recurring stuttering issue).

1953 – The Biden family moved to an apartment in Claymont, Delaware.

1955 – Starts seventh grade at St. Helena's High School.

1956 – Attends Archmere High School. Joe is age fourteen. He graduates at Archmere in 1961.

1961 – Begins college at University of Delaware. He studies Political Science and History.

1964 – Meets Neilia Hunter in the Bahamas while on Spring Break.

1965 – Graduates from UOD with a bachelor's degree.

1966 – Marries Neilia Hunter on August 27, 1966, in New York.

1968 – Graduates from Syracuse University with a Law Degree. He has a draft deferment and is ultimately reclassified, due to asthma when younger, by the Selective Service System as not available for service.

1969 – First child Joseph R. "Beau" Biden III is born.

1970 – Second child Robert Hunter Biden is born.

1970 – Is elected County Councilman (Democratic Party) in New Castle, Delaware.

1971 – Third child Naomi Christina Biden is born.

1972 – In an underdog campaign for the Senate managed by Joe's sister Valerie Biden Owens, he receives an upset victory in November.

1972 – Automotive accident in December kills Joe Biden's wife Neilia and daughter Naomi, the two sons Beau and Hunter suffer injuries but survive. The car Neilia was driving was struck by a tractor trailer.

1973 – Joe is sworn in U.S. Senator from Delaware in January, age 30, the sixth-youngest senator in U.S. history.

1973 – Joe becomes a member of Senate Foreign Relations Committee.

1977 – Joe becomes a member of the Senate Judiciary Committee (he chairs it from 1987 until 1995).

1977 – Joe marries Jill Tracy Jacobs.

1987 – Conducts the proceedings for the Robert Bork nomination to the Supreme Court (votes against the nomination).

1987 – Begins first effort for Democratic presidential nomination, ultimately withdraws, nomination goes to Michael Dukakis.

1988 – Hospitalized in February at Walter Reed Army Medical Center for an intracranial berry aneurysm.

1991 – Votes against authorization for the Gulf War.

1991 – Conducts the proceedings for the Clarence Thomas nomination to the Supreme Court (votes against the nomination).

1994 – Leads the Violent Crime Control and Law Enforcement Act of 1994 (sometimes called the Biden Crime Law) which featured a Federal Assault Weapons Ban. The law expired in 2004.

1999 – Biden supports NATO bombing campaign against Serbia and Montenegro during the Kosovo War.

2002 – Joe's father Joseph Robinette Biden, Sr., dies at age 86.

2007 – Opposes the "Troop Surge" in Iraq. He supports breaking Iraq into a federation of the three main ethnic groups.

2007 – Starts a second run for the presidency, will ultimately withdraw and then accept the vice presidential position with Barrack Obama's campaign.

2009 – Becomes the 47th vice president of the United States (he will be inaugurated for a second term in 2013).

2015 – Beau Biden dies, age 46, losing fight against brain cancer.

2018 – A committee known as *Time for Biden* begins effort to recruit Joe for the 2020 election cycle for the presidency.

2019 – Joe Biden launches his presidential campaign on April 25.

Footnotes

Chapter Two - *Joe's Risky Business*

1. Page 8. https://www.washingtontimes.com/news/2019/dec/30/hunter-biden-file-brief-navy-career/

2. Page 10. https://www.newyorker.com/magazine/2019/07/08/will-hunter-biden-jeopardize-his-fathers-campaign

3. Page 10. https://www.foxnews.com/politics/hunter-biden-ordered-to-pay-monthly-child-support-ending-standoff-over-contempt

4. Page 12. https://obamawhitehouse.archives.gov/

5. Page 22. https://obamawhitehouse.archives.gov/the-press-office/2014/03/18/remarks-press-vice-president-joe-biden-prime-minister-donald-tusk-poland

6. Page 23. https://obamawhitehouse.archives.gov/the-press-office/2014/04/21/background-press-briefing-vice-president-bidens-trip-ukraine

7. Page 25. https://obamawhitehouse.archives.gov/the-press-office/2014/04/21/background-press-briefing-vice-president-bidens-trip-ukraine

8. Page 26. https://obamawhitehouse.archives.gov/ the-press-office/2014/04/22/remarks-press-vice-president-joe-biden- and-ukrainian-prime-minister-arse

Chapter Three - *Bitch Slapped in Moscow*

9. Page 33. "Shellacking" see *15 Years A Deplorable: A White House Memoir*

10. Page 46. https://obamawhitehouse.archives.gov/the-press-office/2011/03/10/remarks-vice-president-joe-biden-and-russian-prime-minister-vladimir-put

11. Page 50. https://obamawhitehouse.archives.gov/the-press-office/2011/03/14/op-ed-vice-president-biden-international-herald-tribune-next-steps-us-ru

12. Page 51. https://cnnpressroom.blogs.ccn.com/2012/03/26/romney-russia-is-our-number-one-geopolitical-foe/

13. Page 51. https://obamawhitehouse.archives.gov/the-press-office/2012/04/26/remarks-vice-president-joe-biden-foreign-policy-campaign-event

Chapter Four - *A Point of Personal Privilege*

14. Page 59. https://obamawhitehouse.archives.gov/the-press-office/2011/08/18/remarks-vice-president-biden-meeting-chinese-vice-president-xi

Chapter Six - *Hollywood, Gays and Guns*

15. Page 85. https://www.youtube.com/watch?v=rLMlb-oNoRM

Chapter Seven - *Joe Will Do Iraq*

16. Page 96. https://www.youtube.com/watch?v=GwZ6UfXm410

17. Page 96. White House's Joining Forces initiative partners with the USO (United Service Organizations) to strengthen military families around the world.

18. Page 98. Soleimani was killed while in Baghdad on January 2, 2020.

19. Page 99. http://archive2.mrc.org/bias-alerts/nbcs-ann-curry-joe-biden-no-wmd-can-us-claim-victory-iraq

20. Page 100. *"... if a JV team puts on Lakers uniforms, that doesn't make them Kobe Bryant."* The New Yorker, Jan. 27, 2014.

21. Page 103. HillTV.com, 9/19/2018

22. Page 105. https://www.teamriverrunner.org/

Chapter Eight - *Everything But The Flying Monkeys*

23. Page 113. The Violence Against Women Act (VAWA) legislation was signed into law by President Bill Clinton on September 13, 1994. It was cosponsored by Joe Biden and Senator Orrin Hatch (R-UT).

24. Page 114. The actress Mariska Hargitay is the youngest daughter of Mickey Hargitay and Jayne Mansfield.

25. Page 114. A "rape kit" is a sexual assault forensic evidence collection method used by medical personnel for gathering facts and preserving the evidence for investigation.

26. Page 115. Joe Biden was elected in Delaware to the New Castle County Council in 1970. He was elected to the U.S. Senate from Delaware in 1972.

27. Page 117. "Middle-Class Joe" released his federal returns in 2019 showing that in 2016, 2017 and 2018, he and his wife Jill had earned $15 million since leaving the Obama White House.

28. Page 118. Eisenhower Executive Office Building (EEOB) is the building adjacent to the White House in Washington D.C.

Chapter Nine - *Donors and Drug Dealers*

29. Page 120. Greece is in Europe, and Turkey in Central Asia. Neither are in the Middle East.

30. Page 121. Which is a city the Greeks also want back from Turkey. Today the city is called Istanbul.

31. Page 121. Chapter 2 of this book discusses how Joe's son Hunter Biden is profoundly involved in Burisma Holdings (see page 7).

32. Page 122. https://obamawhitehouse.archives.gov/the-press-office/2014/05/12/vice-president-biden-and-dr-jill-biden-travel-romania-and-cyprus

33. Page 124. https://www.sigmalive.com/en/news/politics/147994/biden-hopes-cyprus-problem-can-be-solved-by-2016s-end

34. Page 126. https://www.justice.gov/usao-sdny/pr/former-honduran-congressman-tony-hern-ndez-convicted-manhattan-federal-court-conspiring

35. Page 127. *Plan Colombia* was a $10 billion dollar military and social program. It focused on backing the Colombia government which was then in the midst of a violent civil war against the drug-trafficking FARC revolutionaries. The military element of the program drastically reduced violence in Colombia by eradicating FARC strongholds.

36. Page 127. https://obamawhitehouse.archives.gov/the-press-office/2017/01/04/readout-vice-president-bidens-call-president-juan-orlando-hernandez

37. Page 131. http://thegrayzone.com, July 28, 2019.

38. Page 132. https://obamawhitehouse.archives.gov/the-press-office/2016/02/25/blair-house-communique-joint-communique-presidents-el-salvador-guatemala

39. Page 132. https://obamawhitehouse.archives.gov/the-press-office/2014/06/20/remarks-press-qa-vice-president-joe-biden-guatemala

Chapter Ten - *The Greatest Joe Biden Speech You Never Heard*

40. Page 137. James R. Soles (1935-2010) was a professor at the Department of Political Science and International Relations, University of Delaware.

41. Page 138. Beginning in 1991, Biden was adjunct professor at the Widener University School of Law, the only law school in Delaware. The class was so popular it usually had a waiting list for enrollment.

42. Page 139. Joe Biden referred to America's "hard-won position as the indispensable nation" in a speech at the Zbigniew Brzezinski annual prize at the Center for Strategic and International Studies, October 2017. Similar statements have been made by Madeleine Albright, Hillary Clinton, Michelle Bachman, Chris Christie, Jeb Bush, Bobby Jindal, and Marco Rubio.

43. Page 139. Fifteen Years A Deplorable: A White House Memoir By Mike McCormick, page 122.

44. Page 143. As the transcript was not publicly released, the prepared remarks version is on the University of Delaware website where it can be read. A video of Biden's speech is viewable on YouTube. To date it's had just over 200 views: https://www.youtube.com/watch?v=8psLahZUr_c

45. Page 144. https://nypost.com/2019/07/06/biden-apologizes-for-praising-segregationists-in-defensive-speech/

Chapter Eleven - *Trapped*

46. Page 149. The coup attempt in Turkey on August 15, 2016, quickly failed. Erdogan blamed Fethullah Gülen and his followers for organizing the attacks.

47. Page 150. Fethullah Gülen was a popular religious leader and Ottoman scholar in Turkey. He began self-exile in America in 1999. His Turkish passport was revoked by Erdogan's government in 2017.

48. Page 151. https://obamawhitehouse.archives.gov/the-press-office/2016/08/25/remarks-vice-president-joe-biden-and-turkish-prime-minister-binali

49. Page 151. Turkey's Presidential Palace is considered one of the most beautiful presidential architectural structures in the world, built in a style called *Seljuk* which celebrates the Turkish dynasty that conquered Asia Minor during the 11th to 13th centuries.

50. Page 153. https://obamawhitehouse.archives.gov/the-press-office/2016/08/25/remarks-vice-president-biden-and-president-erdogan-turkey-pool-spr

Chapter Twelve - *My Word as a Biden*

51. Page 159. See Chapter Eight, page 111.

52. Page 162. https://obamawhitehouse.archives.gov/the-press-office/2015/05/17/remarks-vice-president-yale-university-class-day

53. Page 164. The National Cancer Moonshot Initiative works to identify new ways to prevent, diagnose, and treat cancer by increasing financial resources and data access between scientists, physicians, philanthropists, and patients.

Index

V

Vietnam War 105, 110
Violence Against Women Act
     (VAWA) 113, 114, 115, 182

W

Wall Street Journal 37, 45, 46, 154
Walter Reed Army Medical Center
     104, 105, 177
Warsaw, Poland 22
Washington, George 31, 141, 142, 143
Washington Post 5, 21, 44, 69, 130,
     153, 154
Weisman, Jonathan 37, 40, 45, 46
West Wing 11, 13, 16, 18, 19, 87, 111,
     161, 171
White House Briefing Room 46
White House Communications
     Agency 73
White House Press Office i
Wilmington, DE 117, 157, 158, 160
World Food Program 10
World Trade Organization 37, 50

X

Xi Jinping, President of China ii, 54,
     55, 60, 62, 63, 65, 66, 71

Y

Yale University Class Day 161
Yanukovych, Viktor 7, 8, 169
Yatsenyuk, Arseniy 26
Yeltsin, Boris 38
Yemen 101
Yildirim, Binali 151
YouTube 85, 96, 184

Z

Zlochevsky, Mykola 15, 20, 21, 122,
     123, 168, 169, 170, 172
Zuccotti Park 145

CPSIA information can be obtained
at www.ICGtesting.com
Printed in the USA
BVHW041923160920
588953BV00017B/678

9 781733 714662